CRAFTS FOR ALL SEASONS

CRAFTS
FOR ALL
SEASONS

LORRAINE BODGER
DELIA EPHRON

ILLUSTRATED BY LORRAINE BODGER

UNIVERSE BOOKS/NEW YORK

Published in the United States of America in 1980
by Universe Books
381 Park Avenue South, New York, N.Y. 10016

© 1975,1976,1977,1980 by Lorraine Bodger & Delia Ephron

80 81 82 83 84 /10 9 8 7 6 5 4 3 2 1

Printed in the United States of America

Designed by Lorraine Bodger

Library of Congress Cataloging in Publication Data

Bodger, Lorraine.
  Crafts for all seasons.

    1. Handicraft.   I. Ephron, Delia, joint
author.   II. Title.
TT157.B662   1980   745.5   79-6410
ISBN 0-87663-318-1
ISBN 0-87663-996-1 pbk.

CONTENTS

Lorraine Bodger and I began our crafts collaboration ten years ago. We opened a crochet business, and sold our fancy crocheted clothes to New York department stores and boutiques. For six months we did nothing but crochet. After filling an order for Bonwit Teller—fifty-four items in less than two weeks—we realized that our love of crocheting was diminishing with every flip of the hook. It would be far wiser to write about crocheting than to market it. So we did. The Adventurous Crocheter, a primer featuring our designs, was published in 1972. After that, we branched out into other crafts, producing a sewing book, Gladrags, and writing a monthly crafts column for teenagers in Ingenue magazine. About that time, Lorraine's craft designs started being featured regularly in Woman's Day magazine.

In 1976, Universe Books published our first of three Crafts Engagement Calendars. Each of the three calendars contained over 50 original craft projects with complete instructions.

We have collected here, in Crafts for All Seasons, our favorites from the crafts calendar designs. There are projects in woodworking, embroidery, sewing, crochet, weaving, patchwork, papercraft, stencil, and shellcraft. There are games and toys, home furnishings and holiday craft projects. To us, the designs in Crafts for All Seasons reflect years of good work and good friendship. We hope you enjoy them as much as we have.

D.E.

EASY WEAVING

This weaving technique eliminates the need to remove the weaving from the loom: The stretcher strips that act as the frame of the loom also frame the finished weaving. You just hang the entire thing—loom, weaving and all.

What you weave and how you weave it is up to you. Any of these materials are fine and a combination of them is recommended: yarn—particularly the shaggy novelty yarns like mohair; strips of fabric; velvet cord; ribbon; bias tape; gold or silver thread; macramé cord; jute; rat tail; raffia. Assemble a collection of these before beginning and use also the following: 4 stretcher strips and the pegs to steady them—the strips can add up to any size square or rectangle; a package of carpet tacks; hammer; yarn needle; cotton string to warp the loom.

Put the stretcher strips together and insert the pegs in the corners. If you don't know how to do this, ask the art supply store to demonstrate when you buy them. Then warp the loom by driving carpet tacks along the top and bottom stretchers, ¼″ apart. Tie the end of the string to the tack in the top left hand corner and wind up and down, keeping the string taut, until you come to the last tack. Tie securely.

Begin weaving. The basic method is over-and-under across the warp. Thread the weaving material on a yarn needle to make the process easier and feel free to take "liberties": Skip strings whenever you want; leave areas of the warp unwoven. Change materials and color as often as desired by cutting the material at the end of a row or even in the middle of a row to make a shaggy fringe.

Hang the weaving by putting 2 nails in the wall and setting the frame over them.

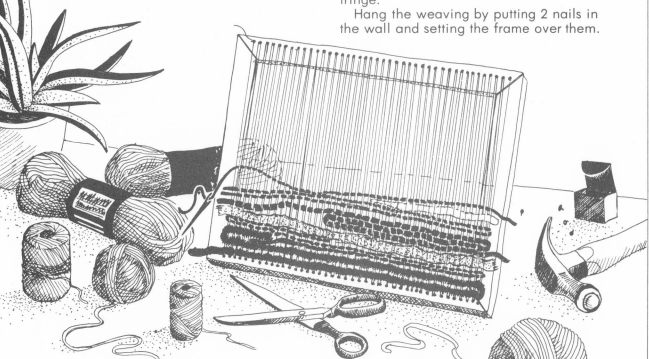

THE BASICS OF EMBROIDERY

Embroidery is done with all kinds of thread—yarn, pearl cotton, crewel yarn, metallic string—but standard embroidery thread, marketed under the name 6-strand floss, is the most common. It is sold at 5-and-10-cent stores, as well as at fancy sewing and needlework shops. Be sure the brand of thread you buy is color-fast. The basic tools of the craft are an embroidery needle, which looks like a large sewing needle, and an embroidery hoop.

When you are ready to embroider, circle the area of the fabric you will be working on with a metal or wooden embroidery hoop. The hoop, which is actually two hoops—one inside the other—holds the fabric firm and flat. Place the inner hoop under the fabric and the larger hoop over the same area on the outside of the fabric. Press the large hoop down around the small one and tighten it.

Cut off a strand of embroidery thread 24" long and roll the end between your fingers to separate the thread into 6 separate strands. Pull out 3 strands and, working with them as if they were one, thread 1 end through the needle and tie a knot in the other end. Now you are ready to embroider—here are the basic stitches.

Note: If you want to change color or are finished, secure the thread by sewing around a few times in the same spot on the wrong side of the fabric, pushing the needle through a stitch and pulling it tight. Cut the thread about 1" from the knot.

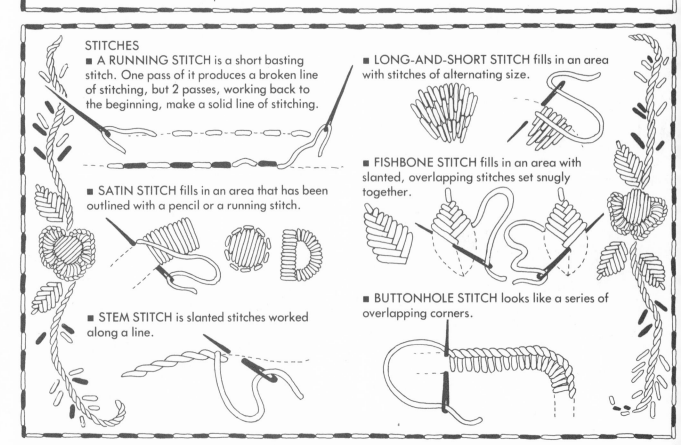

STITCHES

■ A RUNNING STITCH is a short basting stitch. One pass of it produces a broken line of stitching, but 2 passes, working back to the beginning, make a solid line of stitching.

■ SATIN STITCH fills in an area that has been outlined with a pencil or a running stitch.

■ STEM STITCH is slanted stitches worked along a line.

■ LONG-AND-SHORT STITCH fills in an area with stitches of alternating size.

■ FISHBONE STITCH fills in an area with slanted, overlapping stitches set snugly together.

■ BUTTONHOLE STITCH looks like a series of overlapping corners.

FLOWERS FOR THE TABLE

Here are six embroidered flowers to decorate a white tablecloth.

Design an arrangement yourself or follow our suggestions.

TULIP

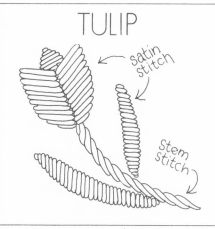

satin stitch

Stem stitch

DAISIES

satin stitch

fishbone stitch

PANSIES

fishbone stitch

long & short stitch

buttonhole stitch

MORNING GLORIES

satin stitch

running stitch

buttonhole stitch

stem stitch

GLADIOLUS

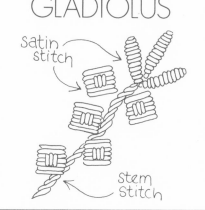

satin stitch

stem stitch

ASTER

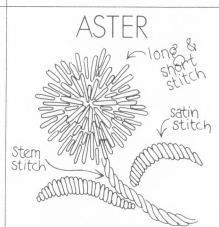

long & short stitch

satin stitch

stem stitch

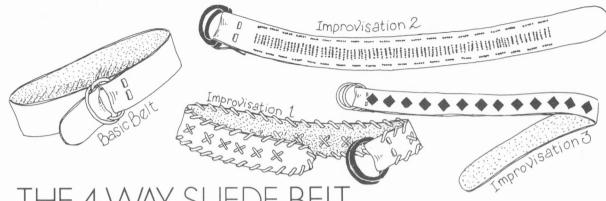

THE 4-WAY SUEDE BELT

Note: Suede is sold by the skin and can be purchased at leather supply stores and many craft and hobby shops.

Materials: Each belt takes one half skin or less of suede; 2 metal belt rings; 1 large darning needle or yarn needle; scissors, felt-tip pen, ruler, fat nail and hammer; extras (see Improvisations).

1. Draw the belt on the suede with a felt-tip pen. The width should be the diameter of the holes in the belt rings; the length is your waist measurement plus 7". Cut out the belt making a curve at one end.
2. Hammer 4 holes in the belt, making each one by putting the nail in position on the leather and giving it a sharp whack. Cut a thin strip of suede to use for a thong. Thread it on a needle and attach the belt to the rings by sewing through the holes.

Now you have the basic belt. Leave it simple or jazz it up.

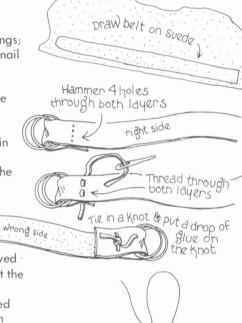

IMPROVISATION 1. Decorate the belt with yarn stitching.

First whip-stitch the edges: Hammer holes along the lengths and curved end of the belt, 1/4" from the edge; thread yarn on a yarn needle, knot the end, and stitch.

Then cross-stitch: Hammer 2 more rows of holes, 1/2" apart, centered on the width of the belt; stop the holes short of the curved end and then make cross-stitches down the center.

IMPROVISATION 2. Decorate the belt with multicolored beads.

Hammer 2 rows of holes 1/2" apart, 1/4" from the edge, down the lengths of the belt, stopping 7" short of the curved end. Then hammer 2 rows of holes centered down the width of the belt, 1/2" apart, stopping 7" short of the curved end. Sew on rows of seed beads or slightly larger beads as shown.

IMPROVISATION 3. Decorate the belt with felt cut-outs.

Cut little squares of felt and glue them with Elmer's Glue in a design down the length of the belt.

CROCHETED HAT

Materials: ½ skein of color A; ½ skein of color B; H crochet hook; yarn needle; 1 piece of shirt cardboard for the pom pom. Abbreviations: single crochet, sc; slip stitch, ss; stitch, st; chain, ch.

1. Begin with color A. Ch 5 and join the first st to the last with a ss.

2. (Round 1) Ch 1 and sc into the ring 8 times. You should have made a full circle around the ring of chs, but if not, add another st. Ss the 1st st of the round to the last.

3. (Round 2) Ch 1. Work around the circle, alternating 1 sc in a st with 2 sc in the next st. When you have come full circle, join the 1st st to the last with a ss.

4. (Round 3-12) Continue to make concentric rounds, increasing the circle. You will have to decide for yourself whether to make 1 st or 2 in a sc of the previous round—the object is to keep the circle full but not overcrowded. Begin each round with a ch 1 and end by joining the first st to the last with a ss.

5. (Round 13-16) Ch 1 and sc in each st of the previous round. Join the first st to the last with a ss.

6. (Round 17-21) Cut the yarn and tie on color B. Continue to crochet as in step 5.

7. (Round 22) Continue to crochet—1 sc in each st of the previous round—but skip every sixth st to reduce the size of the hat.

8. (Round 23) Crochet as in step 5.

9. (Round 24) Repeat step 7.

10. (Round 25-35) Crochet as in step 5, but after row 31, cut and tie on color A. When you finish round 35, cut and end.

11. (Decorative stitching) Thread 2 strands of color B yarn on a yarn needle. Tie the ends of the yarn inside the hat at the 13th round. Pinching that round of crocheting between your fingers on the outside of the hat as shown, whip stitch <u>tightly</u> to form a slight ridge. When you have come full circle, knot the yarn inside the hat.

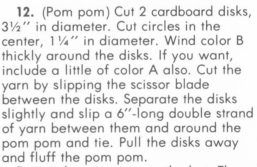

12. (Pom pom) Cut 2 cardboard disks, 3½'' in diameter. Cut circles in the center, 1¼'' in diameter. Wind color B thickly around the disks. If you want, include a little of color A also. Cut the yarn by slipping the scissor blade between the disks. Separate the disks slightly and slip a 6''-long double strand of yarn between them and around the pom pom and tie. Pull the disks away and fluff the pom pom.

Fasten the pom pom to the hat: Thread the ends of yarn on a yarn needle, put the ends through the hole on the top of the hat and tie on the inside.

wind ↓ ←cut

THE ONE-ROOM DOLLHOUSE

This collection of doll furniture in a little one-room house is recycled from food and household containers, scraps of paper and fabric.

THE HOUSE

Cut off the top and side of a cardboard box at least 8" high x 12" wide x 8" deep. Paper the walls with wrapping paper and the floor with construction paper. Using pinking shears, cut an oval rug out of paper or fabric and glue it on the floor.

TABLE

The table top is the bottom of a waxed food container like a yogurt, sour cream, whipped butter or Brussels sprouts container. The base is a 2½" section of a toilet paper or paper towel tube. The four feet attached to the base are cut out of shirt cardboard.

Attach the feet to the base like this: Cut slits of equal length in the legs and tube and slip the pieces together; dab glue on to secure. Paint the base and feet a pretty color.

Glue the base to the circular top. Using pinking shears, cut a round tablecloth out of soft cotton. Glue it to the top and sides of the tabletop.

ARM CHAIR

The seat is made from the end of a cardboard egg carton, the back rest is cut from the top of the carton, and the legs are cones that separated the eggs from one another inside the carton.

Glue the parts of the chair together with Elmer's Glue, then paint the chair. Make 2 little stuffed pillows with pinked edges to fit the bottom and back of the chair.

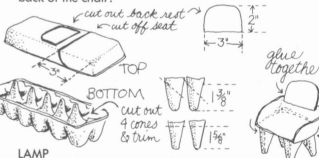

LAMP

The shade is a disposable half-and-half container that comes with your coffee at a restaurant—take one home with you. The base is a spool and the connecting link between the two is a pencil stub, 2¼" long.

Cut the eraser off the pencil stub. Score the eraser end and the inside of the shade with a razor, pin or nail. Push the pencil down into the hole in the spool, dab glue on the scored end and put the shade on. Allow to dry completely.

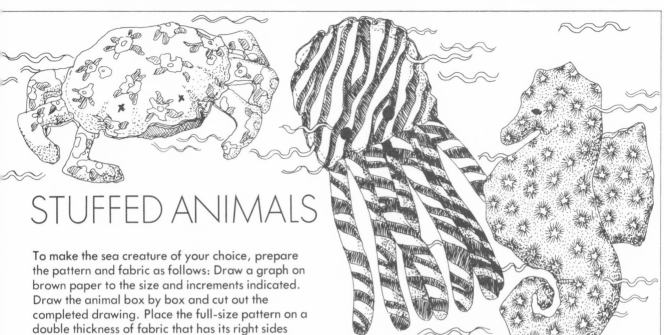

STUFFED ANIMALS

To make the sea creature of your choice, prepare the pattern and fabric as follows: Draw a graph on brown paper to the size and increments indicated. Draw the animal box by box and cut out the completed drawing. Place the full-size pattern on a double thickness of fabric that has its right sides facing. Draw around the pattern with a pencil and cut out the animal outside the pencil line with pinking shears. When there are several tentacles or legs, draw the outline and cut the pattern the required number of times.

CRAB AND OCTOPUS

Prepare the fabric for the body and 8 tentacles of the octopus, 6 legs of the crab. Cut the body 1/2" outside the pencil line and the tentacles (legs), 1/4". With right sides facing, sew the fabric together for each tentacle (leg) along the outline, leaving the straight edge open. Turn right side out and stuff solidly with pillow stuffing to about 1" from the top.

To make the body, notch the curved edges of each piece of fabric and clip the corners off all edges. Turn under the edges 1/2" to the wrong side and iron. Pin the pieces together, wrong sides facing, and pin all tentacles (legs) in place between the edges. Sew around the body, about 1/8" from the edge, catching the tentacles (legs) in the stitching and leaving a 2" opening at the top of the body. Stuff through that hole and sew closed by hand. Embroider eyes.

SEA HORSE

Prepare the fabric for the body and fin of the horse, cutting it 1/4" outside the pencil line. With right sides facing, sew the fabric together for the body along the outline, leaving a 6" opening in the spine. Sew the fin similarly, leaving the long straight edge open. Clip all curved edges. Turn the body and fin right side out. Stuff the body quite plumply and the fin moderately with pillow stuffing. Center the fin in the opening of the body, turn under the cut edges of the spine and pin them together. Sew closed by hand. Embroider eyes on both sides of the head.

1 box = 1 sq. inch

tentacle

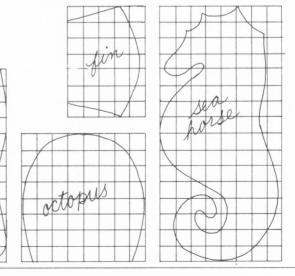

SILHOUETTES

Old-fashioned and quaint, silhouette images convey looks and character in a special, endearing way that a photograph cannot.

Tape a large piece of white shelf paper to the wall. Have your subject sit between the paper and a lamp from which you have removed the shade. Station her so that the light casts the shadow of her profile on the paper. While she sits in this position, trace the outline of her profile with pen or crayon.

Cut the profile out of the white paper. Place it on good-quality black paper and draw around it again in chalk. Cut out the black paper profile and glue it, centered, on a piece of good-quality white paper. Frame or hang as desired.

HAPPY VALENTINE'S DAY

The perfect holiday party cake is pink, delicious and positively hearts and flowers.

Ingredients and materials: 2 chocolate cake layers—one 9" round, one 9" square—baked from your favorite mix or recipe; enough basic white frosting for the 2 layers—use a favorite recipe, mix or canned frosting; decorative frosting ingredients—3 egg whites at room temperature, 1 lb. confectioner's sugar, ½ tsp. cream of tartar; cake decorating set with a round point and a large 6-pointed star (rosette) point; food coloring; toothpick.

1. To make a heart-shaped cake, cut the round layer into 2 half moons and place each half against adjacent sides of the square layer. Frost the cake with basic frosting tinted pink with red food coloring.

2. Use our drawing as a guide and draw the design on the frosting with a toothpick.

3. Make the decorative frosting: Combine all the ingredients, beat at a high speed for 7-10 minutes. Divide the frosting into 4 parts and color each a different pastel color. Keep each bowl of frosting covered with a damp cloth.

4. Decorate the cake in this order, using the round point for all decorations except the rosettes: (1) outline of the 2 hearts, (2) ribbon streamers radiating from points of the hearts, (3) scallop border on top of the cake, (4) outline of large leaves and small leaves, (5) inside of the large leaves (a different color than the outline), (6) rosettes, (7) "Be Mine," (8) scallops around the sides of the cake.

THE COZY KITCHEN

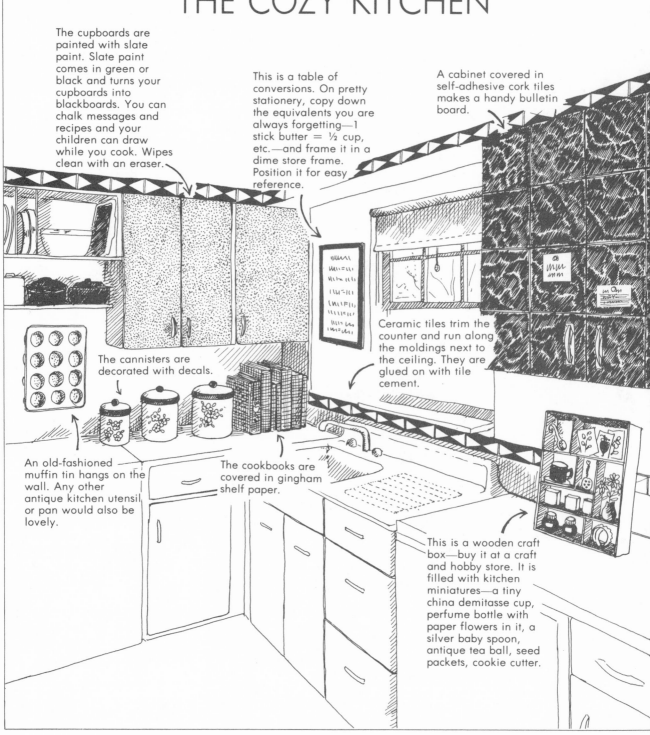

The cupboards are painted with slate paint. Slate paint comes in green or black and turns your cupboards into blackboards. You can chalk messages and recipes and your children can draw while you cook. Wipes clean with an eraser.

This is a table of conversions. On pretty stationery, copy down the equivalents you are always forgetting—1 stick butter = ½ cup, etc.—and frame it in a dime store frame. Position it for easy reference.

A cabinet covered in self-adhesive cork tiles makes a handy bulletin board.

Ceramic tiles trim the counter and run along the moldings next to the ceiling. They are glued on with tile cement.

The cannisters are decorated with decals.

An old-fashioned muffin tin hangs on the wall. Any other antique kitchen utensil or pan would also be lovely.

The cookbooks are covered in gingham shelf paper.

This is a wooden craft box—buy it at a craft and hobby store. It is filled with kitchen miniatures—a tiny china demitasse cup, perfume bottle with paper flowers in it, a silver baby spoon, antique tea ball, seed packets, cookie cutter.

HOW TO GROW BEAN SPROUTS

Rinse   **1st DAY**   Soak

2nd DAY morning   Drain

Spread in container & cover with towels

Remove towels   **2nd DAY** evening   Fill with 1" of water. Let stand.

Drain   Stir

Cover with towels & lid

Materials: a container made of plastic (not clear), china (not stoneware or earthenware) or enamel, large enough to hold grown sprouts and with a large diameter and flat bottom (e.g., plastic storage container, souffle dish); a lid for the container (if it doesn't come with one, a china or plastic plate will do); paper towels; a mixing bowl; a large wire strainer for rinsing beans; ¼ cup or ½ cup beans for sprouting (mung beans, lentils, alfalfa, garbanzos, mustard).

On the evening of the first day, rinse the beans with water. Then put them in a mixing bowl and soak them overnight: 1 cup water for ¼ cup beans; 2 cups water for ½ cup beans.

In the morning of the second day, remove the beans that have not started germinating. These are the ones that did not swell in size, that give off a rotting odor, float on top of the water or have cracked hulls. Drain beans and place them in the growing container, spreading them out evenly. Cover the beans with 4 layers of paper towels, dripping wet. Put on the lid and let stand.

In the evening of the second day, remove towels and fill container with warm water to about 1" above sprouts. Let sprouts stand 10 minutes. Drain container, pouring out the water between the lid and rim or using a strainer if the beans are too small. With a wooden spoon, stir the beans gently to aerate them and move bottom ones to top. Cover sprouts with 4 layers of dripping wet towels, cover and let stand.

In the morning and the evening of the third day, repeat this rinsing process filling the container, draining, stirring and covering with paper towels and a lid. You will find that the sprouts have grown; the husks will be falling off. Remove them as they float to the surface when you fill the container with water, and remove beans that show no sign of sprouting.

On the fourth, fifth and sixth days, harvest if ready; and if not, repeat the rinsing process in morning and evening. To know whether the sprouts are ready for harvest, taste them.

Pointers
◆Keep sprouts moist but not wet. If convenient, sprinkle water on the paper towels in the middle of the day to be sure they don't dry out.

◆ If water collects at bottom of container, sprouts will rot. Drain and turn regularly.

◆ Keep the sprouting beans away from excess heat, like an oven, but at room temperature. Ideal temperature — 70°-80°.

◆Always rinse in warm water.

◆Give them growing room and stack in a few layers.

◆Store harvested sprouts in the refrigerator.

HOW TO MAKE A MEMO BOARD

Materials: foam board, approximately 20″ x 30″; opaque Plexiglas, 19″ x 8″ (or nearest size smaller); fine sandpaper; single-edge razor blade or mat knife; 2 bulldog clips; 1 yd. small print calico, cotton fabric; ¾″ paper fasteners; manual or electric drill with 1/8″ bit; Elmer's Glue; large paintbrush; 4 nails.

With the knife or razor blade, cut the width of the foam board (around 20″) down to match the width of the Plexiglas (around 19″). Place the board on the wrong side of the fabric and outline it with pencil. Cut the fabric about 2″ outside the pencil line and clip the corners as shown. Dilute some glue with a few drops of water in a cup and brush it on the board, covering one side completely. Place the board glue-side-down in position on the fabric. Turn it over and smooth the fabric so it adheres evenly. Apply glue to the back of the board in a 2″-wide margin around the perimeter. Smooth the fabric over the glue, making neat corners. Let dry.

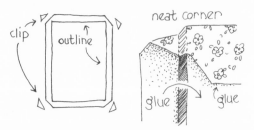

With a pen, mark the 4 corners of the Plexiglas for holes. Clip Plexiglas to foam board, 6″ from the top, and drill through both board and Plexiglas at all 4 locations. Do the drilling over a piece of scrap wood. Secure the Plexiglas to board by slipping paper fasteners through the holes.

Hang the memo board with nails. Write messages on the Plexiglas with water-based felt-tipped markers or washable crayons. To erase, use a damp cloth. Tack your memoranda and mementoes to the foam board with pushpins or thumb tacks.

HOW TO MAKE A RECIPE BOOK

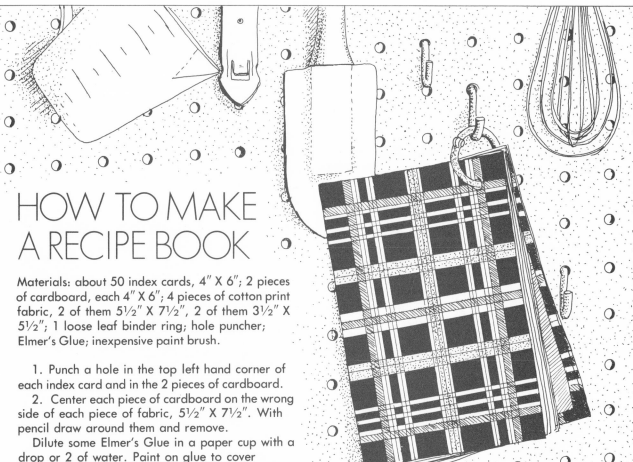

Materials: about 50 index cards, 4" X 6"; 2 pieces of cardboard, each 4" X 6"; 4 pieces of cotton print fabric, 2 of them 5½" X 7½", 2 of them 3½" X 5½"; 1 loose leaf binder ring; hole puncher; Elmer's Glue; inexpensive paint brush.

1. Punch a hole in the top left hand corner of each index card and in the 2 pieces of cardboard.

2. Center each piece of cardboard on the wrong side of each piece of fabric, 5½" X 7½". With pencil draw around them and remove.

Dilute some Elmer's Glue in a paper cup with a drop or 2 of water. Paint on glue to cover completely one side of each piece of cardboard. Glue the cardboard pieces to the fabric, centering them back in place. Smooth the fabric.

3. Clip the corners of the fabric, paint on glue and turn down the edges as shown.

4. Paint on glue to cover completely the parts of each cardboard piece still exposed. Overlap glue on the fabric. Place each remaining piece of fabric in place, centered on the exposed cardboard. Tuck glue under the edges of the fabric to secure them if necessary

5. Snip the fabric on both sides where it covers the hole in the pieces of cardboard. Put the recipe book together on the loose leaf ring, sandwiching the index cards between the fabric-covered cardboard. Whenever you want to write down a new recipe to add to the book or use one that is already in it, open the ring and slip the card out. In the meantime, hang the recipe book on the kitchen wall or pegboard.

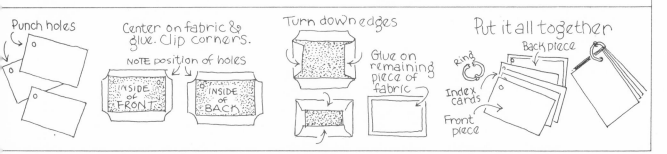

Punch holes

Center on fabric & glue. Clip corners.

NOTE position of holes

INSIDE of FRONT

INSIDE of BACK

Turn down edges

Glue on remaining piece of fabric

Put it all together

Back piece

ring

Index cards

Front piece

MAIL-ORDER CRAFTS

Buying craft supplies by mail is an economical way to shop.
At the mail-order houses listed here, catalogs are free unless otherwise noted.

Dick Blick Co., P.O. Box 1267, Galesburg, IL 61401 (painting, ceramics, weaving, jewelry, batik, silkscreen, linoleum block printing, carving).

Boin Arts & Crafts Co., 91 Morris St., Morristown, NJ 07960 (leathercraft, Indian beading, shellcraft, decoupage, papercraft, printing). Catalog, $1.00.

Boutique Trims, P.O. Drawer P., 21200 Pontiac Trail, South Lyon, MI 48178 (decoupage, jewelry-making). Catalog, $1.00.

Boycan's Craft Supplies, P.O. Box 897, Sharon, PA 16146 (decoupage, shellcraft, beads, findings, macramé, candle-making). Catalog, $1.00.

Brookstone Co., Peterborough, NH 03458 (woodworking tools). Free catalog.

Cake Decorators, 2892 Johnstown Rd., Columbus, Ohio 43219 (baking equipment, tools, & decorations).

Craft Service, 337 University Avenue, Rochester, NY 14607 (batik, picture framing, origami, papercraft, basketry, silvercraft). Catalog, $1.00.

Home-Sew, Inc., Bethlehem, PA 18018 (sewing). Catalog, 25¢.

Lewiscraft, 40 Commander Blvd., Agincourt, Ontario, Canada M1S 3S2 (papercraft, yarns, needle-craft, candle-making). Catalog, $1.00.

Merribee Needlecraft Co., 1517 New York Ave., Arlington, TX 76010 (crewel, embroidery, needle-point, quilting, rug-hooking). Catalog, $1.00.

Nasco Arts & Crafts, 901 Janesville Ave., Fort Atkinson, WI 53538 or 1524 Princeton Ave., Modesto, CA 95352 (decoupage, ceramics, printmaking, painting). Free catalog.

Sax Arts & Crafts, P.O. Box 2002, Milwaukee, WI 53201 (all basic craft tools, woodworking tools, papercraft, ceramics). Catalog, $3.00.

School Products Co., Inc., 1201 Broadway, New York, NY 10001 (weaving). Catalog, $1.00.

Some Place, 2990 Adeline St., Berkeley, CA 94703 (equipment & yarn for spinning, weaving, lace-making, macramé, rug-hooking, tapestry). Yarn samples, $1.00, Catalog, 50¢.

Standard Doll Co., 23-83 31 St., Long Island City, NY 11105 (doll-making). Catalog, $2.00.

Stewart Clay Co., P.O. Box 18, 400 Jersey Ave., New Brunswick, NJ 08902 (ceramics, enameling).

Sun Ray Yarns, 349 Grand St., New York, NY 10002 (yarns for knitting, crocheting, weaving). Sample card, $4.50.

Tandy Leather Co., P.O. Box 791, Fort Worth, TX 76107 (leather-craft). Free catalog.

Vanguard Crafts, 1701 Utica Ave., Brooklyn, NY 11234 (jewelry, beads, enameling, candle-making, shellcraft, decoupage, ceramics, printing, stained glass, Indian beading). Catalog, 50¢.

The Yarn Depot, Inc., 545 Sutter St., San Francisco, CA 94102 (needlecraft, embroidery, crocheting, knitting).

HANG IT ON A HEART

Use this wall unit in the kitchen as a rack for utensils or hang it next to your dresser to display and store necklaces and bracelets.

Materials: 1 piece of ¼" plywood, at least 8" square; coping saw; medium and fine sandpaper; electric or manual drill with 3/16" or ¼" bit; hammer and thin nail; 3 ½" cup hooks with ¼" shafts (see drawing); acrylic paints and paintbrushes; quick-drying lacquer or shellac and an inexpensive brush; scraps of felt; Elmer's Glue; 2 pieces of narrow velvet or satin ribbon, each 20" long.

Draw a heart pattern on paper, using the graph as a guide. Cut out the pattern and outline it on the wood. Cut out the heart with a coping saw. Drill 2 holes in the heart as shown on the graph, using the drill and a 3/16" or ¼" bit. Sand all rough edges, first with medium and then with fine sandpaper.

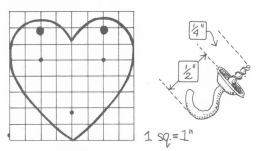

1 sq. = 1"

Mark the locations of the cup hooks, and with hammer and nail, tap pilot holes at the 3 points. Screw in a cup hook at each point. Note: The sharp tips of the hooks will come through the back of the wood slightly. Do not be concerned. Coats of paint and lacquer will blunt the tips and they will be covered with felt hearts.

Paint the entire heart with 2 coats of acrylic paint, allowing each coat to dry thoroughly. Then paint on decorations or apply some decals.

Finally paint on 2 coats of shellac or lacquer, allowing each coat to dry thoroughly.

When the lacquer is completely dry, cut 3 small hearts from the felt scraps and glue them to the back of the heart, covering the points of the cup hooks.

To hang the heart, tie a piece of ribbon to each hole at the top of the heart and then tie the ends in a bow. Balance the bow over a nail or hook on the wall.

THE BASICS OF GRANNY SQUARES

Granny squares, little patches of crocheting of equal size and shape, are traditionally sewed together into colorful afghan blankets and throws. But, in recent years, the versatility and charm of granny square crocheting has been put to good use in fashioning clothing, pillows, and other home furnishings. The basic technique is easy for a beginning crocheter to master.

ABBREVIATIONS: st, stitch; ch, chain; dc, double crochet; ss, slip stitch.

1. Make a ring of 6 chs joined together with a ss.
2. (Round 1) Ch 2 and dc, putting the hook into the center of the ring and pulling the yarn through the center and not through a st.

Make all the dcs in this round through the center of the ring. Ch 2 and dc 2 times—repeat this sequence 2 more times. Ch 2 and join the last st to the first st with a ss. End of Round 1.

3. The ch sections of Round 1 become the corners of the square in the next round. Ss under the next chs around, skipping the dcs. Each time you complete a round, ss like this to set up for the next round.

4. (Beginning Round 2) Ch 2 and dc. All dcs in the granny square appear above chs of the previous round of sts and crochet them by pulling the yarn <u>under</u>, not through, the ch sts.

Ch 2 and dc 2 times right next to the dcs you just made. You have just made a corner. Ch 1.

5. Dc twice at the next section of chs. Ch 2 and make 2 more dcs right next to the last ones. Ch 1. Repeat this step 2 more times. Join the last st to the first st with a ss. End of Round 2.

6. (Beginning Round 3) Ss under the next chs around. Ch 2 and dc; ch 2 and dc 2 times right next to the dcs you just made. You have just turned a corner. Ch 1.

7. Dc 2 times at the next ch sections of the previous round. Those 2 dcs are a section between 2 corners. Ch 1.

8. Now make your corner section; 2 dcs, ch 2 and 2 dcs. Then the in-between section: ch 1, 2 dcs, ch 1. Repeat this step 2 more times, then join the last st to the first st with a ss to finish the round.

9. Another round would look like this. The corner sections are the same, but the in-between sections increase. Keep making rounds until the square is as large as you want it.

DECORATING WITH GRANNY SQUARES

RUGS
Crochet large squares in heavy twine, cord or jute. Sew together with a whip stitch.

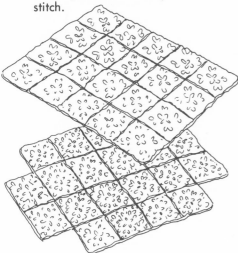

BEDSPREADS & THROWS
Crochet in wool or synthetic worsted to make fine afghan throws. Use sport yarn for baby blankets and Speed-Cro-Sheen or cotton yarn for bedspreads.

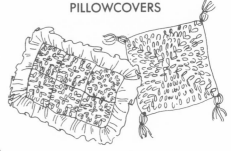

TABLE MAT & RUNNERS
Crochet small squares in delicate pearl cotton, Knit-Cro-Sheen, Speed-Cro-Sheen or in a combination of them.

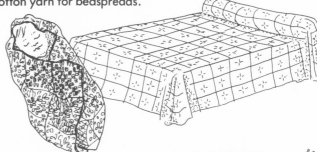

PILLOWCOVERS

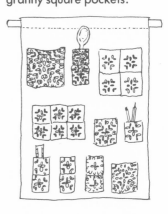

CATCHALL
Make the backing of canvas, denim or duck and sew on granny square pockets.

CURTAINS
Use granny squares to trim curtains or as inserts to make curtains wider or longer.

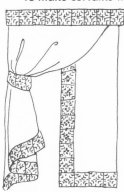

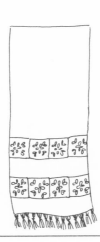

REVERSE GLASS PAINTING

Reverse glass painting is a traditional American folk art. A picture is painted on the back of a piece of glass and framed, with the unpainted side facing the viewer.

To make your own reverse glass painting, you will need the following: 1 ready-made picture frame that is fitted with glass and a cardboard backing piece; an assortment of poster paints—red, blue, yellow, green and white will do nicely since you can mix other colors from these; 1 paintbrush; a plate on which to mix colors; 1 piece of white paper with which to back the painting if none is included with the frame; a favorite picture (in color) approximately the size of the framed glass. When choosing a picture, consider using an outdoor scene, a quilt pattern, a photographed still-life, a painting, a geometric pattern, Persian miniature.

Begin by removing the glass from the frame and cleaning it thoroughly. Denatured alcohol works well. Center the glass over your picture and tape it to the picture with 2 small pieces of tape. You will remove the tape when you want to paint the areas it covers, but meanwhile it will hold the glass and picture securely together.

Now simply copy the picture by painting on the glass. Mix colors as you need them, keeping several glasses of water handy for rinsing your brush.

Important: The colors that you set down first will be the ones that will show on the other side of the glass. Colors painted over the first color will not show. For example, if you are painting a blue sky with clouds, paint the white clouds first and then fill in with blue sky. If, instead, you fill in completely with blue and then add white clouds, the clouds will not be visible on the other side of the glass.

When you are finished painting, let the paint dry completely. Then place the painting in the frame with the unpainted side facing the viewer. Back it with white paper, cutting the paper down, if necessary, to fit. Add the cardboard and clamp them in. Hang the picture.

SWEET SMELLS

POMANDER

A pomander is a lime, lemon or orange covered with whole cloves. The cloves should be inserted in the fruit so closely that the heads of the cloves touch. Use a pushpin to help you—press the point of the pushpin into the fruit, remove it and push the clove in where you made the hole. When the fruit is covered in cloves, tie a pretty ribbon—striped, plaid or embroidered—around the pomander.

TANGY SACHET

Mix together 1 tsp. mint leaves, 1 tsp dried orange peel (it comes grated into tiny bits) and 6 whole cloves. Divide the mixture between 2 sachets. Make each of the sachet bags like this.

Using light cotton, voile, batiste, nylon or a similar pretty sheer material, cut 2 fabric rectangles, 2¼" x 3", with pinking shears. With wrong sides facing, sew 3 sides together, ⅜" from the edge. Fill the bag with half the mixture and sew up the 4th side. Decorate by sewing on a ribbon bow.

SWEET SACHET

Crush 1 large vanilla bean with a hammer, breaking it into bits and pieces. Mix with 12 crushed cloves and 4 tsp. dried basil. Divide the mixture among 3 sachets. Make each sachet bag like this.

Using pinking shears and a light cotton or similar synthetic (not a sheer fabric), cut a fabric circle, 6½" in diameter, making points around the edge, or cut a plain circle, 5½" in diameter. Place the sachet mixture in the center on the wrong side of the circle and close the sachet bag one of 2 ways.

■ Bring up the fabric around the mixture and tie tightly with a piece of yarn or ribbon.

■ Sew a short basting stitch in a circle about 1¼" from the edge. End the thread on the outside (right side) of the fabric. Pull the thread to gather the fabric tightly so that none of the mixture can escape. Fasten off the thread.

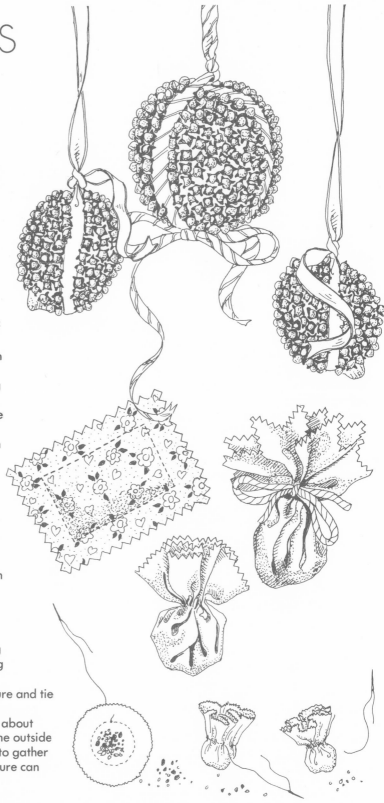

HOW TO MAKE A PHOTO ALBUM

Materials: firm cotton fabric; heavy cardboard; single-edge razor blades; scissors; Elmer's Glue; paper cup; inexpensive paint brush, about 1½" wide; paper punch; embroidery thread; sharp embroidery needle; steel ruler; a pad of interesting textured paper like charcoal paper, oatmeal or craft paper (sold at art supply stores).

1. With a razor blade and ruler, cut 2 pieces of cardboard 9¼" x 6" and 2 pieces 1¾" x 6". With scissors, cut 2 pieces of fabric, 13" x 7½".

2. Dilute several tablespoons of glue in a paper cup with a few drops of water. Paint on glue to cover completely one side of each piece of cardboard. Center the boards on the fabric, separating the smaller and larger boards by ¼" but keeping the tops and bottoms even. Make certain the fabric is smooth.

3. Clip the corners of the fabric, paint on glue, and turn the edges in, making neat corners.

4. Cut 2 pieces of fabric, 6" x 11¼", for the inside linings of the cover. Turn the edges under ¼" and iron. Completely cover the exposed cardboard on each cover and its fabric border with a coat of diluted glue and press the lining fabric smoothly in place, keeping the edges turned under. Apply a little extra *un*diluted glue at the edges. Let dry thoroughly.

5. Cut sheets of paper 5¾" x 11". Punch 4 holes in each sheet 1⅝" from the end.

6. Stack the book—the back cover with the lining side up, the pages and then the front cover with the lining side down. Important: Each cover, as you may remember, is made of 2 pieces of cardboard separated by ¼" of fabric. The paper should be placed between the covers so that the punched holes are directly above the separation (in the case of the back cover) and directly below the separation (in the case of the front cover). This is necessary so that when you sew the book together, you can sew between the cardboard pieces and not through cardboard.

Sew the book together with embroidery thread, tying it on top with a double knot.

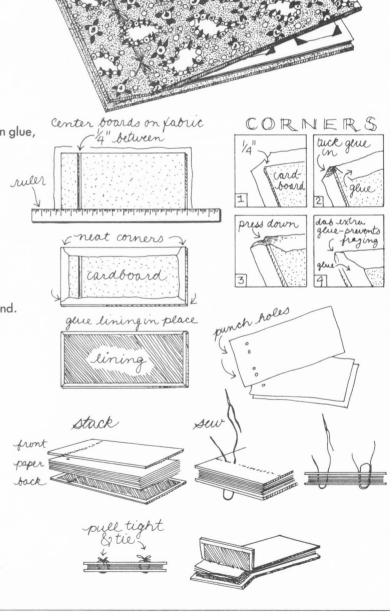

Center boards on fabric
¼" between
ruler

CORNERS
¼"
card-board
1
tuck glue in
glue
2
press down
3
dab extra glue-prevents fraying
glue
4

neat corners
cardboard

glue lining in place
lining

punch holes

stack
front
paper
back

sew

pull tight & tie

BEAUTIFUL BOXES
For jewelry, treasures, letters, notions

Use a wooden box from a handicraft store or, for the sequinned design, you can use a cigar box—just ask for an empty one at a tobacco shop.

SHELL BOX OR PEBBLE BOX
Materials: sea shells or pebbles, Elmer's Glue.

Wash and dry the shells or pebbles. Completely cover the top of the box with a mosaic pattern. Lift up each shell or pebble one by one, apply glue to the bottom and put back in place. Let the glue dry for an hour. Line the interior of the box—see below.

SEQUINNED BOX
Materials: felt, sequins-on-a-string, Elmer's Glue, small paint brush, paper cup. Optional: ribbon, felt scraps, other decoratives.

Measure each exterior surface of the box, except the bottom. Cut a piece of felt to exact measurements for each surface. Dilute glue in a cup with a drop or two of water. Brush glue liberally on the box and, as each surface gets a complete coating, cover with felt. If you have any trouble getting felt to adhere, thicken the diluted glue with more glue. With undiluted glue attach sequins to the edges of the top of the box. Decorate the box with additional sequins, ribbon, felt appliqués or whatever strikes your fancy.

INTERIOR OF THE BOX
Materials: pretty wrapping paper, small paint brush, Elmer's Glue, paper cup.

Measure the interior surfaces of the box. Cut a piece of wrapping paper to exact measurement for each surface. Put each   piece in place to see if it fits. Trim if necessary. Dilute glue in a cup with a drop or two of water. With the brush, cover interior surfaces completely with glue: first the bottom and put paper in place; then each side and apply paper; then the top only if you are using a cigar box.

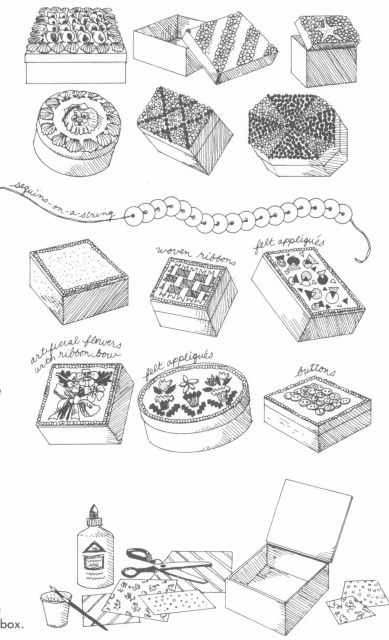

sequins-on-a-string

woven ribbons

felt appliqués

artificial flowers with ribbon bow

felt appliqués

buttons

MONOGRAMS

Embroider monograms on clothing and household items in any way you like.

To transfer the letter you want to embroider, trace it from this page onto tracing paper. Place the tracing paper on top of a small piece of dressmaker's carbon and position them both in place on the item to be embroidered, carbon facing down on the fabric. Draw over the letter with a ball point pen. The carbon will transfer the letter to the fabric. Then embroider the letter, copying one of our designs or inventing your own.

ABCDEFI
GHJKLM
NOPQRS
UH̤R̤MS̤T̤Z
TVWXY

TINSEL ART

Outline a picture with opaque ink, fill in the areas with transparent paint and the background with opaque black or white paint. Back the painting with crumpled foil so that the transparent areas, set off by foil and surrounded by darkness, shimmer like mother-of-pearl.

1. Take the frame, bend the clamps up and remove the backing cardboard and white paper. Throw the white paper away. Clean glass on front and back without removing it from the frame.

2. With the back of the glass facing you, center and tape the picture to the front of the glass so the picture is facing you too, through the glass.

3. Outline the picture on the back of the glass, drawing in details as well as the whole. Use the black drawing ink and pen. Practice first—you can always wipe your practice lines off the glass.

4. Spray ink lines several times lightly with Krylon Spray.

5. Use the small and medium brushes to paint in the outlined areas with transparent paint. The trick, in creating the transparency, is thinning the acrylic paints with gloss medium, not water. The thinned colors will appear weak and even somewhat colorless when you paint them on; however, they will look quite bright when backed with foil. Paint quickly; do not stroke over and over or you will disturb the ink lines. Note: Use white sparingly when mixing colors since it tends to counteract the effect of the gloss medium.

6. Paint in the background. Black and white are very effective, but any color can be used. The paint must be full strength, diluted only a bit with water if necessary. Paint right up to the ink outlines, using the small brush for small areas and the large brush for surrounding areas. Apply 3 coats of paint, allowing each to dry before applying another.

7. Cut a piece of foil about 1" larger than the frame on all sides. Crumple it carefully and spread it out again without tearing it until it is about the same size as the glass. Put a few dabs of gloss medium on the painted side of the glass (it works as a glue) and press the foil down on the glass, flattening the foil without smoothing out the wrinkles. Put the frame back together.

Materials: picture frame from the 5-and-10 (it comes with glass and backing cardboard); simple decorative print or picture of flowers, birds, butterflies or folk art designs (this picture is the basis of the painting and it should be small enough so that you can copy it on the glass and still have a generous border); penholder and plain pointed nib; black drawing ink; Krylon Crystal Clear Acrylic Spray; 3 paintbrushes—small, medium, and large; tubes of acrylic paint—a good selection includes cadmium yellow medium, cadmium red medium, ultramarine blue, Hooker's green, dioxazine purple, titanium white, mars black; gloss polymer medium (it is mixed with the paint to make it more transparent); aluminum foil; jars of water.

HOW TO MAT A PICTURE

A complete mat consists of 2 pieces of heavy board.
One piece has a window that frames the picture (a print, photograph or drawing).
The other is used as a backing piece—the print is taped to it.

Materials: A picture to frame, anything 9″ x 12″ or smaller; mat board—smooth or pebble finish in white, off-white or one of the various colors available; metal ruler; mat knife with brand new blade; 6-H pencil; paper tape, 1½″ wide or wider.

To decide the measurements of the top piece of board, which will be the frame, here is some information that you need to know. The width will be the width of the picture plus the width of the side borders of the mat. The height will be the height of the picture plus the height of the top and bottom borders. When measuring the picture itself, you must make an arbitrary decision on how much of the plain border around the photo or print you want to show. Important: On a mat, the left, right and top borders are always the same measurement, but the bottom border is ½″-1″ wider.

So to make the calculation, you must decide the width of the mat border: 2″ for the sides and top and 2½″ for the bottom is a good all-purpose size. A more generous mat, however, may give the picture more presence: For instance, 3″ for the top and sides and 3¾″ for the bottom. It's a matter of taste and you should decide for yourself what will look best on your picture.

When you have calculated the overall dimensions of the top piece, use the mat knife and metal ruler to cut mat board to those measurements. Then draw the border and carefully cut out the window. Here's the cutting trick: When you cut the window, first jab the mat knife into the corners, making indentations at right angles. Then when you reach a corner while making the complete cut, the mat knife falls into already-made holes and doesn't overshoot the mark.

Cut the backing piece next. It is the size of the top piece minus ¼″ of the overall width and 1/8″ of the overall height.

Cut a piece of paper tape about ½″ less than the overall width. Lay the top piece face down and the backing piece face up on a table—top edges pressed firmly together. Wet the tape and apply as shown. Do not move the mat boards until the tape is dry. When the tape dries, it serves as a hinge.

Slip the picture in the frame and position it correctly, centered at the window. Carefully lift the top piece and tape the print at the top 2 corners to the backing board.

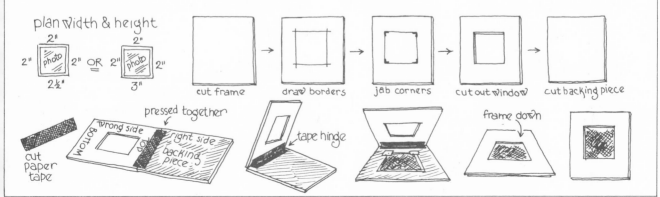

plan width & height

2″ | 2″
2″ | photo | 2″ OR 2″ | photo | 2″
2½″ | 3″

cut frame → draw borders → jab corners → cut out window → cut backing piece

cut paper tape — pressed together — wrong side — bottom — right side — backing piece — tape hinge — frame down

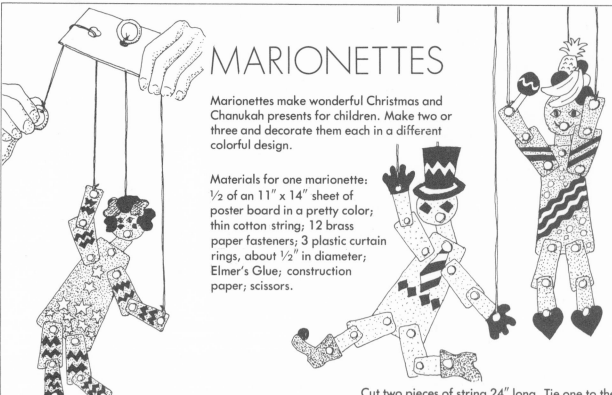

MARIONETTES

Marionettes make wonderful Christmas and Chanukah presents for children. Make two or three and decorate them each in a different colorful design.

Materials for one marionette: ½ of an 11″ x 14″ sheet of poster board in a pretty color; thin cotton string; 12 brass paper fasteners; 3 plastic curtain rings, about ½″ in diameter; Elmer's Glue; construction paper; scissors.

Cut the parts of the marionette out of poster board and punch holes as shown. Round off all the corners. Put the marionette together with paper fasteners.

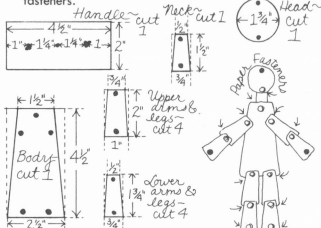

Cut a piece of string 15″ long. Tie one end to the hole at the top of the head, slip the other end through the center hole in the handle and tie to a ring. The marionette is now suspended from the handle.

Cut two pieces of string 24″ long. Tie one to the end of each arm, attaching it through the punched hole. Then slip a brass fastener into the hole in each arm to weigh them down. Now you are ready to fit each string to the handle, and this takes a bit of fussing.

Work on one string at a time. First slip the string through the hole in the handle. Then tie the end to a ring (don't knot it because you will have to unfasten it in a second). Lift the marionette up by the handle and straighten out the attached arm. The string is either too long—it gapes—or is too short—it pulls the arm up. Retie the string to the ring, shortening or lengthening it as required. Hold up the marionette by the handle again and see if the string is the right length. If not, adjust until it is. Then secure the string to the ring with a double knot, dab some glue on the knot and cut the end short. Attach the other string in this manner.

Decorating the marionette: Each marionette you make should be decorated differently. Cut stripes, hearts, stars, zigzags, diamonds, polkadots, etc. out of brightly colored construction paper and glue in a design. Cut a head of hair or a hat and glue in place on the head, covering up the punched hole in the process. You might outfit the puppet in crazy shoes or gloves.

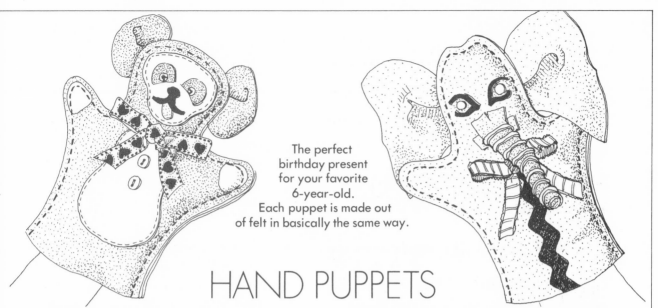

The perfect
birthday present
for your favorite
6-year-old.
Each puppet is made out
of felt in basically the same way.

HAND PUPPETS

With a pencil on paper, draw closely around an adult hand as shown. Cut out and use the paper pattern as a template. For each puppet, draw around the template twice on felt and cut out . Designate one of these "hands" as the front of the puppet and trim it as follows.

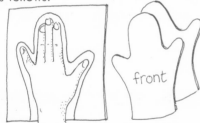

PANDA BEAR TRIMMINGS: Cut paws, tummy, and face out of a contrasting color of felt. Tack these parts in place on the front of the puppet with fabric glue. Sew the face and tummy to the front by hand or machine. The paws will be sewed on later when the front and back of the puppet are stitched together. Sew on sequins for eyes, 2 small buttons on the tummy and a ribbon bow at the neck.

ELEPHANT TRIMMINGS: Cut eyes out of a contrasting color of felt. Glue them with fabric glue to the front of the puppet. Then make the elephant trunk out of the same color felt as the body. First roll up a piece of felt, 3½" X 2½", so that one end is wider than the other. Glue the trunk along the edge so it cannot unroll—the side with the edge will be the underside of the trunk.

Snip ½" slits in the wider end to make the tabs that will attach the trunk to the elephant's body. Cut narrow strips of a contrasting color of felt and glue them on the trunk as trim. Spread the tabs and glue each one to the elephant's front to attach the trunk.

Finish trimming the elephant by sewing a 4½" piece of medium-sized rickrack up the front and topping it with a ribbon bow.

When trimming is completed, cut ears for the puppet as shown. Glue a little tuck in each of them.

Place the front of the puppet on the back, sandwiching the ears in place between them. Be sure the ears are tucked in far enough to be secured when you sew the puppet together. Sew the front to the back with a sewing machine, stitching approximately ¼" from the edge. Leave only the lower edge open for the child's hand to go in.

THE BASICS OF SEMINOLE PATCHWORK

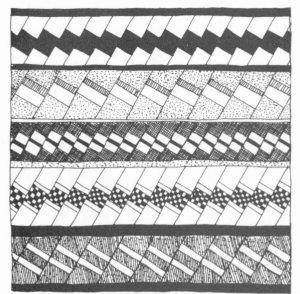

The intricate look of this traditional craft of the Seminole Indians is achieved by sewing narrow bands of fabric horizontally to a wide band of fabric, cutting it into vertical strips and rearranging the pieces on the diagonal.

To simplify and speed up the process—but not compromise the results—use cotton fabric in combination with seam binding, grosgrain ribbon, embroidered and plaid ribbon and bias tapes of any width. Do all sewing on a sewing machine. Piece the finished patchwork bands together into fabric as the Seminole Indians do or use them separately as trims for clothing or household furnishings.

THE BASIC TECHNIQUE

Cut a band of cotton fabric, 3" to 7" wide, for the foundation. (Remember that you will lose width when the strips are turned diagonally and trimmed down.) Sew a horizontal ribbon and tape decoration to the band of fabric, according to which design you prefer. Decoration possibilities:

■ embroidered ribbon centered on a wider strand of solid color ribbon or bias tape (or narrow bias tape or seam binding centered on a wider ribbon)

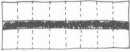 

■ a single strand of ribbon or bias tape

■ a strand of ribbon bordered on each side by narrow bias tape

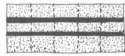 

■ 2 narrow tapes or ribbons stitched ½" apart

■ a wide ribbon or seam binding bordered on 1 edge by a narrow ribbon

Cut the decorated band of fabric into narrow strips of equal size, allowing a ¼" seam allowance on each side of the strips. Rearrange the strips on the diagonal and sew them together. Cut off the points to make the top and bottom edges straight. Sew to another band of Seminole patchwork or turn under the top and bottom edges and use as trim on clothing or furnishings.

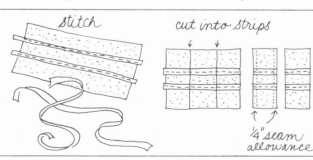

stitch · cut into strips · ¼" seam allowance

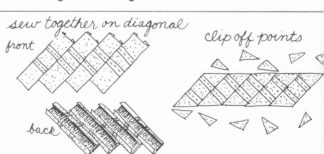

sew together on diagonal · front · back · clip off points

DECORATING WITH SEMINOLE PATCHWORK

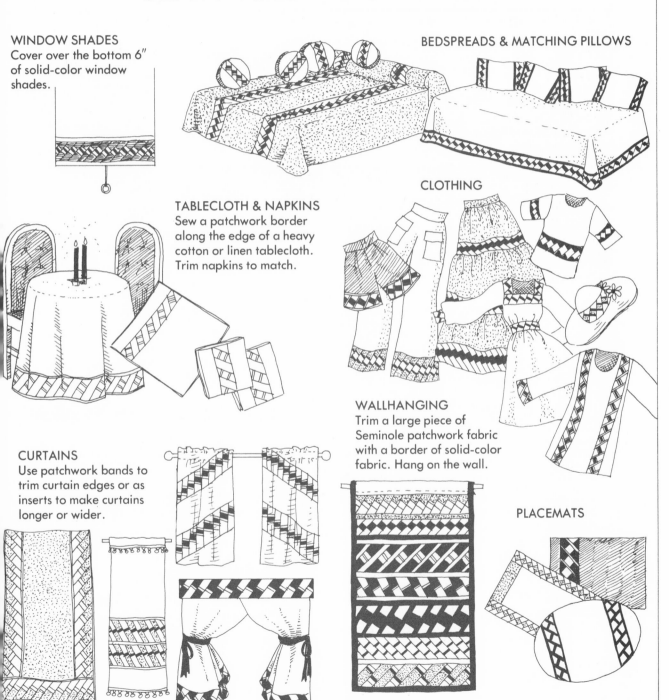

WINDOW SHADES
Cover over the bottom 6″ of solid-color window shades.

BEDSPREADS & MATCHING PILLOWS

TABLECLOTH & NAPKINS
Sew a patchwork border along the edge of a heavy cotton or linen tablecloth. Trim napkins to match.

CLOTHING

WALLHANGING
Trim a large piece of Seminole patchwork fabric with a border of solid-color fabric. Hang on the wall.

CURTAINS
Use patchwork bands to trim curtain edges or as inserts to make curtains longer or wider.

PLACEMATS

MINIATURE GENERAL STORE

This drawing shows the general store, stocked and open for business.

Here are instructions for building the store, shelves and counter. On the opposite page find out how to make the miniatures that furnish it— bins of potatoes and onions, brooms, sacks of flour and sugar, bolts of calico and a ladder.

The Store
Materials: ¼″ plywood cut into 4 pieces—11½″ x 15″ for the floor, 10″ x 15″ for the back wall, 10″ x 11¾″ for each of the 2 side walls; fine sandpaper; Elmer's Glue; very thin nails or brads about ½″ long; paint or stain; varnish.

Sand all 4 pieces of wood, especially on the cut edges. Glue and nail the floor and back wall together as shown. Then glue and nail on each side wall.

Paint or stain the inside and/or outside of the store however you wish. One possibility: Paint the inside walls a medium blue gloss enamel, stain the floor a dark brown, and paint the outside a dark green enamel. Regardless of whether you paint or stain, cover the entire store with 2 coats of varnish.

The Counter
Materials: 2 strips of balsa wood, each 1/8″ thick, at least 2½″ wide and at least 18″ long; X-acto knife; Elmer's Glue; fine sandpaper.

From one strip of wood, cut 2 pieces 8″ x 2″. Glue together on a flat surface as shown. Let dry completely before assembling with other pieces.

From the remaining strip, cut 2 pieces—one 8¼″ x 2½″ and another, 6 1/8″ x 2½″. Glue together at right angles as shown. Let dry completely.

Glue the 2 sections together perpendicular to each other and let dry. From the scraps, cut 2 end pieces to fit, sanding them down to fit snugly. Glue as shown. Let dry.

Both shelves and counter may be painted, stained or left natural.

The Shelves
Materials: 9 strips of balsa wood, 1/8″ thick, 1″ wide, at least 15″ long; X-acto knife with new blade; Elmer's Glue.

Draw lines where the shelves will go: On each wall, draw one line 5½″ from the top edge; a second, 3½″ from the top edge; and a third, 2″ from the top edge.

Cut 3 shelves, each 15″ long, for the back wall. Pick up the store and turn it so it rests on its back. Apply glue to one long edge of each shelf and place each in position on a pencil line, perpendicular to the back wall. Let dry.

Now glue shelves to the side walls: Rest the store on one side, cut shelves to fit, apply glue to one long edge of each shelf and place in position. When the glue dries, turn the store on its other side and attach the last 3 shelves.

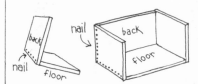

Vegetable bins. Cut 5 pieces of balsa wood and glue together as shown. Fill with potatoes, onions or apples molded from self-hardening clay.

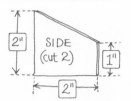

BACK = 2" x 2"

FRONT = 1" x 2¼"

BOTTOM = 2¼" x 2¼"

Ladder. Make it from 2 8" strips of balsa wood joined by 2" strips.

Stool. Working in balsa wood, cut and sand the edges of a circle 1" in diameter. Cut 3 short legs, sand the ends to slight angles and glue to underside of circle.

Brooms and mops. Cut a 3½" strip of balsa wood for each handle. Cut dozens of 2" lengths of pearl cotton or string. Glue and tie them to the handle as shown.

STOCKING THE STORE

General Instructions

All kinds of odds and ends are used in making miniatures so use your imagination and feel free to make substitutions for specified materials.

Balsa wood items are made from 1/8"-thick strips and pieces. Balsa may be carved or rounded off carefully with an X-acto knife. It can also be sanded with fine sandpaper.

The molded items are made from self-hardening clay. Some brands come in colors and some can be painted. Take your choice or use baker's clay if you know how to make it.

Sacks of flour, sugar and rice. Cut rectangles of muslin. Sew 2 rectangles together on 3 sides, turn inside out, stuff with cotton and sew closed. Label with a felt tip pen.

Bolts of cloth. Wrap strips of tiny-printed cottons around pieces of balsa wood ¾" x 2¼". Glue the end of the fabric down.

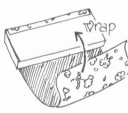

Canned goods: Saw ¼" and ½" dowels into short pieces. Sand the ends. Cover with bits of colored paper or paint with acrylic paint.

Skeins of yarn.

Plates, mugs, bowls. Shape from self-hardening clay. Painting is optional.

Strings of onions. Shape onions from clay. String them together with a needle and thread before the clay dries. Secure bottom end with a drop of glue and glue the top end to the underside of the shelf.

Food. Shape long breads, cakes, fruits and vegetables from self-hardening clay. Paint if desired. Display food in appropriate containers: a large button makes a cake plate; tiny baskets hold carrots; a balsa wood slab is a cheese board.

Bundles of wood. Tie 2" lengths of twigs together with string. Stack in a 6-bundle pile.

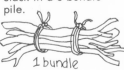

1 bundle

Button cards. Glue seed beads to tiny rectangles of stiff paper.

INTRODUCTION TO ART & CRAFT PAPERS

This page will acquaint you with the wide variety of art and craft papers and their relatives, metallic foils and boards. All those listed are sold at art supply stores and other stores, when indicated.

Newsprint paper.
Newspapers are printed on it, but don't run out to retrieve yesterday's sports section. Buy clean pads of white newsprint and a similar paper called oatmeal. Newsprint is smooth, while oatmeal paper has a texture something like oatmeal. Inexpensive and utilitarian, both papers are ideal for children's art activities—painting, drawing, potato prints—as well as for wrapping gifts.

Charcoal, pastel and watercolor papers. Elegant substitutes for construction paper, the textures of these papers range from fine-grained to pebbly and are favorites for painting and drawing. Charcoal and pastel refer not to the paper color, but to the sticks of chalk the artist uses on them. In fact the special advantage of these papers is their exquisite, subtle colors: heathers, muted roses and blues, brilliant turquoise and emerald green.

Flint Paper. Colored on one side only, flint paper has a slick, shiny, high-gloss finish. Buy it in individual sheets or packages of assorted colors and use for paper-cutting, holiday decorations, cards or wrapping paper.

Aurora Paper. The color is printed on one side only and that side has a matte finish. Ideal for cards and invitations.

Origami Paper. This square paper is customarily used in the Japanese art of paper folding. It comes in packages of 30 or more sheets in a rainbow of colors. Use for a variety of papercrafts: paper-cutting and folding, cards, paper doll clothes, decoupage.

Metallic papers. They are colored on one side only with gold, silver, or copper ink. Most of these papers are stiff, but metallic foil paper has the malleable quality of ordinary aluminum foil. Often available at craft and hobby stores.

Rice Paper. Ideal for making block prints and for mounting dried flowers and leaves, rice paper is a light-weight, translucent and expensive paper.

Tableau paper. Similar to rice paper, but tableau paper is less delicate and considerably less expensive. Its main talent is absorbency, which makes it perfect for paper dyeing, rubbings and block printing.

Bristol board. It comes with a smooth surface, called plate finish, or a slightly textured surface, called vellum finish. More important, it comes in 4 different weights (thicknesses)—1-, 2-, 3- and 4-ply. One-ply is thin like typing paper—nice for the endpapers of a book; 2- or 3-ply would make fine invitations—they are the papers that engraved invitations are printed on; 4-ply is heavy like shirt cardboard and would be ideal for making a box.

Foam Board. It is a light-weight foam core laminated between 2 pieces of shiny white paper. Ideal for bulletin boards, building material for children's toys, miniatures, posters or display backdrops.

Boards. Inexpensive posterboard, oaktag and railroad board are very heavy papers, most commonly known for their use as prom posters. Heavier stiff boards that can stand by themselves—called illustration board or mat board—are used for display and for matting pictures and prints. All of these boards come in an assortment of colors and, in the case of mat and illustration boards, in smooth or pebble finish.

A JAPANESE BOOK

Materials: 2 pieces of 1-ply Bristol board, each 5½" x 8½", for the covers; 2 pieces of colored tissue paper, each 7½" x 10½", for covering the outside of the covers; 2 pieces of tissue paper, each 5¼" x 8¼", for lining the inside of the covers; 40-50 pieces of white typing paper (called bond paper), cut to 5½" x 8½" for the pages of the book; a spool of pearl cotton (a thin string sold at the 5-and-10); 3 thin nails; large embroidery needle; Elmer's Glue; 1 large paintbrush and 1 small paintbrush; 2 bulldog clips.

1. Cover and line each cover with tissue paper.

Iron the tissue with a dry iron set at low to medium heat. Center the front cover on a 7½" x 10½" sheet of tissue. Draw around it with pencil, remove and clip off the corners of the tissue paper. Dilute some glue with water in a paper cup and, with the large brush, coat 1 side of the cover with glue. Place the cover back in place on the tissue, glue-side-down. Immediately turn over and smooth out the tissue. Turn the cover back over to the white side and brush diluted glue along the edges. Bring the tissue up over the glue and smooth it out, making neat corners. With a small brush, glue down any loose corners and edges.

Brush diluted glue on the uncovered side all the way to the edges. Center a 5¼" x 8¼" piece of tissue paper on the glue and smooth it out. When the cover is almost dry, press it under a stack of heavy books. Remove when dry.

2. Stack the pages and attach them together at the corners.

Tap the pages firmly into alignment and clip them together with bulldog clips. Cut 2 1" squares of typing paper. Fold the squares in half and snip along the folds as shown. Brush diluted glue on the squares and apply them to the corners.

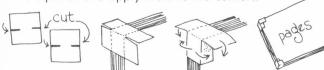

3. Put the book together—the 2 covers with the pages sandwiched between.

Mark one cover at 3 points, A, B and C as shown. This will be the front cover. Stack it, the pages and the back cover together, aligning them

perfectly. Then, working on a surface of heavy cardboard or wood, hammer a nail through the entire book at each marked point. Wiggle the nails around in their holes to loosen them and to widen the holes slightly. Leave nails in place.

Thread an embroidery needle with a 1-yd. piece of pearl cotton. Remove the middle nail and bring the needle up at the middle hole (B) leaving 18" of pearl cotton remaining on the other side.

Bring needle down at A, removing that nail, and up and around the spine and back down at A again. Bring the needle over the top of the book and down at A once more. Finally bring the needle up at B, pull the thread out of the needle and leave it.

Remember that 18" of pearl cotton is still hanging down. Thread it on the needle. Bring the needle around the spine and down at B. Then bring it up at C, removing the last nail, and around the spine and up at C again. Finally, bring the needle around the bottom of the book and up at C. Pull the needle off the pearl cotton.

Tie the 2 ends together snugly at B—make a double knot and secure it with a drop of glue. Snip ends very short.

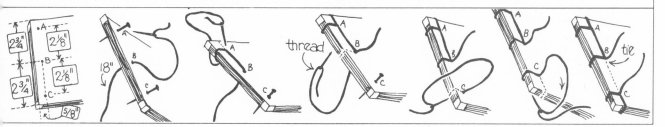

CRAFT KITS

Introduce a friend to craft satisfaction. Give a homemade craft kit for a present.

BEAD AND TRIM KIT
Fill the compartments of an egg carton with an assortment of beads and trims. Here is one possible combination: a packet each of sequins, studs, seed beads, pearl beads, wooden beads and rhinestones; 3 yards of flat lace; 3 yards of rick-rack; 6 buttons; 1 yard fancy ribbon; a few small appliqués.

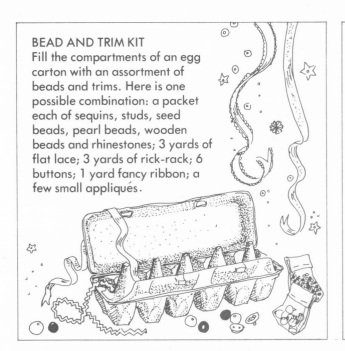

DECOUPAGE KIT
An empty cigar box from a pipe and tobacco shop can be the gift box and the object to be decorated with decoupage. Fill it with the craft materials: cut-outs for the decoupage montage (cut them out of magazines, catalogs, wrapping paper, etc.); Elmer's Glue to apply the montage; a small jar of the decoupage finish, Liquitex Gloss Polymer Medium; and a 1/2"-wide paint brush to apply it.

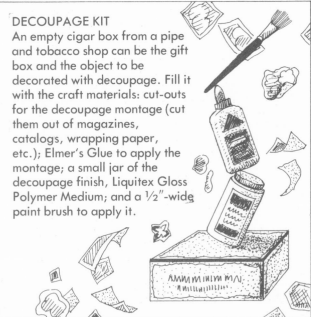

SANDPAINTING KIT
Buy a clear plastic planter—one that will be a pretty container for the sandpainting. Into it put four bags of colored sand, a pointy stick, crochet hook or knitting needle and a plastic spoon. Tie a big red ribbon around the planter.

EMBROIDERY KIT
The ingredients—a wooden embroidery hoop, an embroidery needle, an assortment of embroidery threads, and a pretty item to be embroidered like a tablecloth, 8 solid color dinner napkins or a plain, pretty peasant shirt. Bag them in plastic and tie with a ribbon.

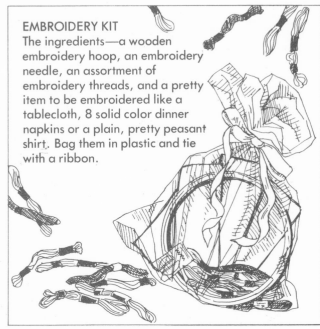

CRAFT KITS

CROCHET KIT

Into a clear plastic shopping bag, put the crochet essentials—2 or 3 hooks in different sizes, 3 skeins of yarn, a yarn needle and a basic paperback book on the subject. Tie ribbons through the handles of the bag.

STENCILCRAFT KIT

Buy a plain wooden box at a craft and hobby shop. Rest the bottom on the top and inside put 3 small stencil patterns cut from lacquered, brown, paperbag paper; a small stencil brush; a small paint brush; and 4 jars of poster paint. Tie a ribbon around it.

CANDLEMAKING KIT

The ingredients—1 lb. household paraffin, stearic acid, candle wick, a small package of crayons for coloring the candles and a package of paper baking cups, muffin size, to use for candle molds. Pack them all in an inexpensive aluminum pot that your friend can melt wax in.

SAMPLER KIT

In a string bag, place 1 piece of fine linen, about 8" X 10", with the cross stitch pattern already printed on it. Add a picture frame to fit and embroidery materials—a needle, an assortment of threads and a hoop.

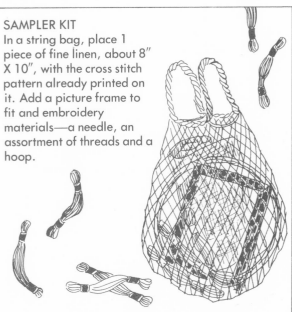

THE BASICS OF CREWELWORK

Crewel is a kind of embroidery. The stitches are standard embroidery stitches, but the distinctive "crewel" look is achieved by embroidering traditional floral and nature designs in many colors of wool thread on a neutral background fabric.

The yarn to use is crewel wool, a 2-ply twisted yarn. You need a wooden or metal embroidery hoop to hold the fabric taut and a crewel needle. Crewel needles are similar to embroidery needles; they come in sizes 1 through 12—the higher the number, the finer the needle. Unbleached linen or fine wool is the ideal fabric for crewel work. If this is unavailable, buy an all-natural fabric—cotton is fine—in a neutral shade like white, ivory or beige.

Running Stitch is a short basting stitch. One pass of it produces a broken line of stitching, but 2 passes, working back to the beginning, makes a solid line of stitching.

Satin stitch fills in an area that has been outlined with a pencil or a running stitch.

Preparing for Crewelwork

Circle the fabric with the embroidery hoop. Cut a piece of crewel wool 24" long. If you would like especially delicate embroidery, roll the wool between your fingers and separate it into two separate strands; plan to embroider with each strand separately. If not, leave the wool thread as is. Select a crewel needle with an eye just large enough to receive the thread. Thread the needle and tie a knot in the other end of the thread. You are now ready to do crewel embroidery.

Note: If you want to change color or are finished, secure the thread by sewing around a few times in the same spot on the wrong side of the fabric, push the needle through a stitch and pull it tight. Cut the thread about 1" from the knot.

A **French knot** is a bumpy knot made by winding the thread around the needle.

Long-and-short stitch fills in an area with stitches of alternating size.

HOW TO MAKE A
CREWEL CHAIR CUSHION

Materials: Crewel embroidery materials (read previous page) fabric for the cushion—wool, linen or cotton in white, ivory or beige; tracing paper; Polyfil or other synthetic pillow stuffing; needle and thread; 2 store-bought tassels; 4 strands of gros grain or velvet ribbon, each ½''-1'' wide and 10'' long; dressmaker's carbon.

Draw a paper pattern of the chair seat and cut it out along the pencil line. Fold the fabric in half and outline the pattern on it. Cut the fabric, ¾'' outside the pencil line, through both layers of material. One layer is the top of the pillow and one, the back. The crewelwork will be done on the right side of the top piece only.

Plan a design for the cushion using our motif. Possibilities: Embroider it in all 4 corners, in the center, in a circle, or as a border. When you have planned the design, transfer the motif to the fabric.

Copy the motif on tracing paper. Pin it in position on the fabric with a piece of dressmaker's carbon sandwiched between. Be sure the fabric is right side up and the carbon is face down. Then carefully retrace the design, pressing down firmly with either a pencil, knitting needle or other pointed object.

Embroider the fabric using instructions on the previous page as a guide. Then turn it into a pillow: Put right sides of both pieces of fabric together; sew as shown; turn right side out and sew ribbon ties and tassels into the corners; stuff the cushion and stitch the last side by hand.

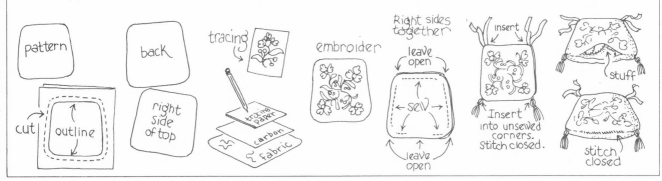

HOW TO MAKE BRAIDED RUGS

These rug designs are made from rounds of braided rug sewn together in different arrangements.
The directions for making each round are identical. Make as many rounds as you need, and then add the border.

PREPARING THE MATERIALS

Braided rugs are made of strips of fabric. The easiest fabrics to work with are thin, firm ones like cotton, voile, soft denim and flannel, but you might also want to use soft wool or jersey.

Collect all your pieces of fabric and iron them. Snip and tear (or cut, if it's easier) the fabric along the selvage at these intervals: 1½" for heavy cotton and wool; 2" for medium-weight fabrics; 3" for voile and other thin fabrics.

Turn under the raw edges of each strip and steam iron them. Hold the iron in one hand and turn down the top raw edge of the fabric with the forefinger of the other hand and turn up the bottom raw edge with the thumb. Iron as you fold.

MAKING EACH ROUND

Sew the ends of 3 strips together. Braid the strips, folding each one in half as you work. Folding keeps the ragged edge tucked firmly out of sight.

When you have braided to the end of a strip, sew a new one on. Important: If all your strips run out at the same time, unbraid and cut back 2 of the strips so that all 3 strips end at different lengths. If you attach 3 new strips—or even 2—at the same place, you will end up with a large lump in the rug.

Braid until you have a braided piece about 2 yards long. Cut the ends even and pin them together.

Now sew and lace the braid into a round. Begin by gathering the loops together at the stitched end of the braid with a needle and a double strand of heavy-duty thread. Then use a blunt needle—a yarn needle, for example—threaded with thin string or light-weight cord to lace the braid into a round: Anchor the cord in the back by tying it to one of the loops; bring the

needle to the front and lace; work from side to side (not over and over) and go through as many loops as possible.

When you have about 8" left to lace, unbraid the strips about 5". Cut each end off on a steep diagonal. Rebraid for about 3" and tuck each end through a loop close to the edge of the round so it comes out on the back. Finish lacing and, finally, secure the tucked-in ends on the back with stitching.

SEWING THE ROUNDS TOGETHER

When you have made as many rounds as you need, sew them together with a needle and heavy-duty thread. Sew on the back, at the points of contact that occur when the rounds are all laid out in final position.

ADDING THE BORDER

Braid 3 strips, beginning with 8" of each strip cut steeply on the diagonal. Continue braiding, adding strips when needed, until you have several yards of braid. Pin the ends together.

Thread the tapered ends of the braid through the loops on the main body of the rug and sew to the back. Then lace the braid to the rug, working around the rounds as closely as possible. Make the border as wide as you like. Just add strips and braid as you go. End the border with tapered-off strips.

RECYCLE

PAPER LOGS

Paper logs can burn almost as long as regular logs. You can make several logs out of one daily newspaper.

Fold 8 sheets of newspaper in half. Soak them in water, roll them up and tie securely with string. Let the log dry a day or two. When it is completely dry (anything less will result in smoldering, not burning), burn it in your fireplace.

HERB GARDEN

Save a cardboard egg carton and eggshells. Prick holes in the bottom of each half shell with a pin and place one in each compartment of the egg carton. Put a few grains of gravel in each shell. Fill half way up with plant soil and sprinkle on a few herb seeds like chervil, mustard, basil, fennel or thyme. Add more soil. Water lightly and place on a window sill where they will get lots of sun. Transplant to small pots or outdoors when they are well started.

BRAIDED RUG

Save old stockings and panty hose with runs in them. When you have a large collection, begin the rug.

Cut the legs off the panty hose and throw the tops away. Cut all legs in half lengthwise. Divide the strips into groups, and dye each one a different color. Then sew 3 strips together at the top and braid them. As each strip in the braid ends, sew another strip to it. It makes a prettier rug if the strips are different lengths and so end at different times because the color change in the rug will have more variety. When the braid is 1 or 2 yards long, start winding it into a circle or oval and overhand stitch it together. Keep braiding and winding until the rug is as large as you want it.

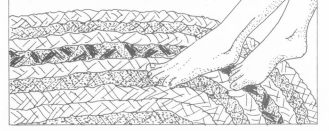

CHILDREN'S CRAFT BOX

This box of collage materials is welcome on rainy days.

Into a large box put a pair of scissors, Elmer's Glue and a package of construction paper to do the collages on. To give the box a good start, take a tour around the house and collect things from each room. From the bathroom, toss in a few cotton balls, Q-tips and empty toilet-paper rolls; from the kitchen, toothpicks, empty paper-towel rolls, small empty packages (raisins, pasta, spices), a few paper napkins, a handful of dried beans and pasta, labels from empty cans; from closets and drawers in the bedrooms, discarded costume jewelry and pieces of shirt cardboard; from the living room, old magazines, catalogs, funnies; from the sewing room, bits of rickrack, fabric scraps, beads, ribbon, yarn; from the office, old used envelopes, labels, last year's Christmas cards, old postcards, index cards, scrap paper.

Now you have enough supplies to last a few rainy days. From now on, keep the box well stocked—when you start to throw something away, throw it instead into the craft box.

FINGERWEAVING

Fingerweaving is weaving with all the pleasure and none of the paraphernalia. Since no loom is necessary, minimal preparation and costs are involved. One of the simplest fingerweaving techniques is the Peruvian flat braid. With it a beginner can turn out a beautiful and surprisingly elaborate wall-hanging with no trouble at all.

THE BASIC TECHNIQUE

All the threads hang vertically—they make up the warp. The weaving is done in one direction, always in the same direction: You take the outside thread on the left or right side (this is the weft) and weave it over and under across the warp. Take the next outside string on the same side and repeat, reversing the over-under sequence. Continue in this manner. After a thread has been woven across to the other side, you just let it hang down and become part of the warp, weaving through it with the next weft.

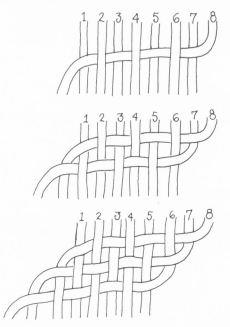

HOW TO MAKE A WALLHANGING

Select threads in a variety of colors, types and textures. Suggestions: cord, string, jute, rug yarn, chenille, braid. Cut strands about 48" long. The number you cut will depend on how wide you want the hanging. In the color and design order you desire, attach them to a holder that will give you tension while you weave. Suggestions: Tie them to a wire hanger; clamp them between the sides of a skirt hanger; clip them to a clip board.

Begin weaving, working always in one direction—from left to right or right to left, whichever is easier.

DESIGN POINTERS

■ You can vary the look of the hanging by varying the tightness of the weave. To make it tight, push the weft up snugly right after you weave it; to make it loose, weave loosely and don't push up the weft.

■ Divide the weaving into groups and weave separately; then combine them again. Regroup in as many different arrangements and as many times as you want. Just be sure you always divide into groups containing an even number of threads.

■ Decorate the weaving with beads. Slip them up the weft thread, weave it and place the bead along the weave where you want it.

When the weaving is as long as you want, detach it from the holder. Sew across the top 2 or 3 times with a sewing machine to secure the threads. Trim the top to about 1½", turn under and hem. Leave the bottom in a fringe—trim to desired length, at least 4".

To hang, sew wide bias tape across the back or sew loops to the top. Slip a dowel through and balance on nails.

RING TOSS GAME

The entire family can play. Score 5 points for landing a ring on an outside peg and 10 points for a bulls-eye. If you get 2 rings on the same peg, double your score. Three rings on the same peg and you can triple it.

Materials: a piece of ½" plywood, 21" x 24"; 5 ½" dowels, each 6" long; 3 pieces of ½" nylon rope, each 15" long; medium and fine sandpaper; a roll of 1½"-wide Mystic tape; a 21"-long piece of 1-by-2; enamel paint and paintbrush; electric drill with ½" bit; hammer and nails; turpentine for cleaning the brush.

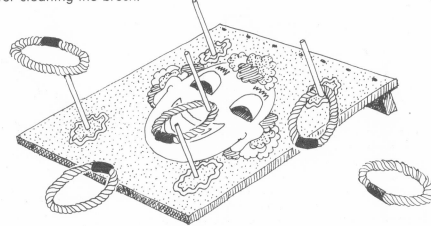

Sand the rough edges of all pieces of wood and dowels. Mark the large piece of wood (the gameboard) for peg holes. Drill the holes, working over a piece of scrap wood. Nail the 1-by-2 to the top back edge of the game board.

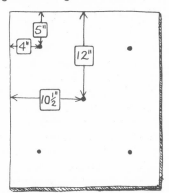

Paint the game board in bright colors. You might design an archery-type target—painting circles around the holes where the pegs will go—or do a star design. You might also paint a landscape with the pegs as important sites or pitfalls or draw a silly clown face—the bullseye is the big red nose. Below each peg hole, indicate the points awarded. Paint the dowels. Let dry.

Dab glue in the drilled holes and insert the dowels. Let dry.

Make each of the 3 rope rings like this: Hold the ends of a 15"-length of rope end to end; tightly wrap the ends flush together with Mystic tape. This job is easiest if you have help—one person holds the rope end to end while another wraps the tape around several times. When the rings are made and the paint is dry, you are ready to play. Post a scorecard on the wall near the target to keep a running tabulation and proclaim the reigning champion.

THE CLOWN ON THE FLYING TRAPEZE

Materials; 5 pieces of cotton fabric—each a different bright color or pretty print; felt scraps in assorted colors; 6 pom poms cut from medium or small ball-fringe; narrow plastic bangle bracelet; fabric glue; paper for making patterns; pinking shears; Polyfil or other synthetic stuffing.

1. Enlarge the patterns on brown paper or typing paper, using graphs as guides. Cut out the patterns.

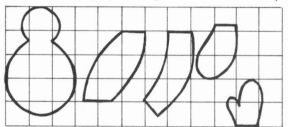

1 sq. = 1"

2. Each of the 5 parts of the clown—body, legs, arms—is made of a different piece of fabric. Fold each piece in half with right sides together. Use pencil to outline a pattern on each piece, copying the arms and legs twice. Cut out along outlines with pinking shears, through both layers. Turn each pair of cut-out pieces so their wrong sides are together.

3. The felt scraps are for the shoes and gloves. With pencil, outline each pattern 4 times on felt, using a variety of colors. Cut out with scissors and glue together with fabric glue in pairs.

4. Glue and sew 3 pom poms to one of the pieces of fabric cut for the body. Glue and sew a pom pom to each of the shoes.

5. Sew the shoes to the legs and gloves to the arms by sandwiching the felt pieces between the fabric pieces as shown, and then sewing around 3 sides of the arm or leg.

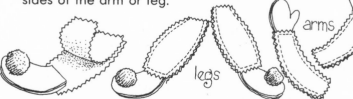

arms

legs

Stuff each leg with Polyfil—pushing the fiber in with the eraser end of a pencil—stopping about ¼″ from the open end. Stuff each arm stopping about ¼″ from the open end.

6. Sew the arms and legs to the body, sandwiching them between the 2 layers of the body. Stuff the body up to the neck. Then sew up the sides of the head, leaving enough unsewn at the top so that you can still get the eraser in to stuff it. Stuff the head and then sew up the last little open section.

stuff · sew · stuff · finish sewing · sew

7. Cut 2 identical triangular hats from felt and sew them to the head, sandwiching the cords of the last pom pom in the top. Be sure the cords get caught in the stitching. By hand, sew eyes and a mouth on the clown's face.

8. Fold the felt gloves over the plastic bangle bracelet and sew them securely. Suspend the bangle by a cord or ribbon over the baby's bed or from the light fixture in the nursery or playroom.

WHAT SHALL WE GIVE THE BABY?

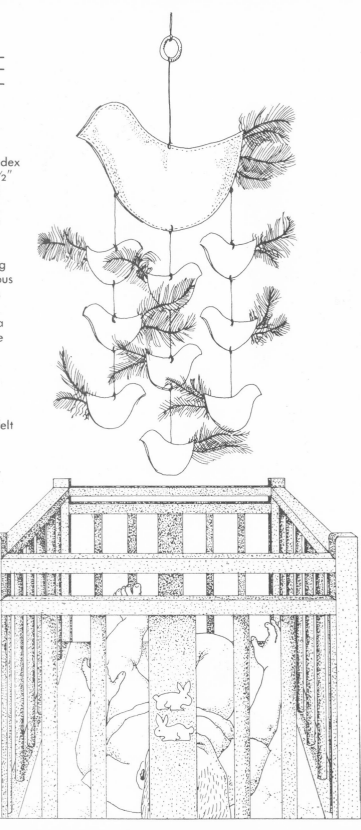

Draw a graph on a piece of stiff paper or an index card 2″ high x 2½″ wide. Make the graph lines ½″ apart. Draw the baby bird square by square and cut it out. This is the template.

To make the nine baby birds, draw around the template 18 times on pretty colors of felt and cut out each bird shape. Make each small bird by gluing two pieces of felt together and sandwiching several feathers between their tails. Use a generous amount of Elmer's Glue inside each tail and press firmly to keep the feathers in place.

Draw a graph pattern with lines ½″ apart on a piece of stiff paper 5½″ high x 7″ wide. Draw the large bird square by square and cut out the template. Draw around it on 2 pieces of felt. Cut out each bird shape. Sew the 2 pieces of felt together, leaving a 1¾″ opening at the tail end. Stuff the bird lightly with a pillow stuffing like Polyfil or foam chips. Put glue on both pieces of felt inside the tail and slip several feathers in. Press together firmly and let dry.

Join the birds together in the formation shown, using a large needle threaded with embroidery thread. Add a thread and a plastic ring at the top and hang it from the ceiling on a hook to suspend it over the crib.

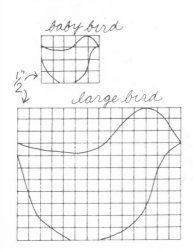

baby bird

½″

large bird

WHERE DOES YOUR GARDEN GROW?

Why not use a beautiful bentwood hat stand, a wall coat rack, or a wooden collapsible clothing rack as a tree for hanging plants. Or make a display of an assortment of plants in an unusually-shaped or unusual container like an old violin case, a hat box, a wicker picnic basket or your child's now outgrown little red wagon. Children's toys make terrific plant holders—consider a fire engine planter or a wooden train with each car containing a tiny plant. Plants can be grown in large sea shells—a conch, for instance—or in your pretty kitchen equipment: Any brightly-colored enamel pot will make a lovely planter and a colander is perfect—it even has holes for drainage. Where does your garden grow? Just about anywhere!

HOW TO MAKE A BEADED FLOWER NECKLACE

Materials: 3 14-oz. or 8-gram packets of rocaille beads—1. multicolor assortment, 1 dark color, 1 light color (i.e. dark blue and aqua, dark green and lilac, black and mint green); 1 packet beading wire; 1 yd. narrow satin ribbon; heavy-duty thread; thin needle to string beads; scissors; ruler; small piece of felt; Elmer's Glue.

1. (Making the petals) Each petal is made as follows.

Cut a piece of beading wire 9" long. String on 2 of the assorted color beads, 10 of the dark color beads and 2 more assorted beads. Push the beads down on the wire until they are 2" from one end. Form a loop of the beaded section and twist the wire to hold the beads in place.

Now work with the long end of wire. String on 2 assorted beads, 20 dark color and 2 more assorted. Form the beaded section into a loop around the first loop and twist to hold.

Working with the long end again, string on 4 assorted, 25 dark and 4 more assorted. Form into a loop around the second loop and twist to hold.

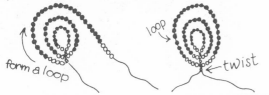

Repeat this step to make 4 more petals of dark color beads and 5 petals of light color beads.

2. (Putting the flower together) Stack 5 petals, alternating the colors and twist all the stems together. Do the same with the remaining 5 petals. Put 1 stack on top of the other, twist the 2 big stems together and spread the petals out, overlapping them. Curl the stem around on the back of the flower, cut it down and glue a piece of felt to the back.

On the front of the flower put 1 or 2 drops of glue in the center where the wires show. Drop a few beads (assorted colors) on the glue to conceal the wire—the glue will show now, but it will dry clear.

3. (Attaching the ribbon) Cut the ribbon in half. Attach each half to the middle loop of a petal as shown.

UKRAINIAN EGG PAINTING

Follow this batik process to make elegant Easter eggs in the Ukrainian folk art tradition. It works basically like this: paint the eggs with melted wax, dye them and remove the wax—the waxed areas will resist the dye and the design will appear as a combination of dyed and undyed areas. Painting with wax requires precision and concentration so do not be surprised if you have to experiment with a few eggs before you develop a facility.

Materials: hard-boiled eggs at room temperature, 1 metal spoon, candle in holder, candle stub, thin water-color paint brush, matches, paper towels, foil, food coloring, vinegar.

Cover the work areas with foil. Cut a small piece of wax off the candle stub and put it in the spoon. Light the candle that is in the holder and hold the spoon above the flame. While the wax melts, swish the brush around in it so the brush gets warm and waxy. Set the spoon down when the wax is melted—there should not be too much wax in the spoon or it will spill.

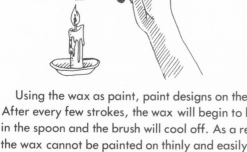

Using the wax as paint, paint designs on the eggs. After every few strokes, the wax will begin to harden in the spoon and the brush will cool off. As a result, the wax cannot be painted on thinly and easily. As soon as this happens, put down the egg and hold the spoon above the flame, swishing the brush in the wax. Then start painting again. You have to keep alternating between egg-painting and wax-melting in this manner.

When the eggs are painted, prepare the dye according to instructions on the food coloring package. But, instead of using boiling water for the dye, use hot tap water. Test the temperature of the water by dipping some hard wax in it—the dye should *not* melt the wax. If it does, let it cool until it doesn't.

Place the egg in the dye. Remove when the color is satisfactory and dry by blotting the egg with a paper towel.

Remove the wax from the egg by holding the egg next to the flame. As the wax melts bit by bit, wipe it off with a paper towel.

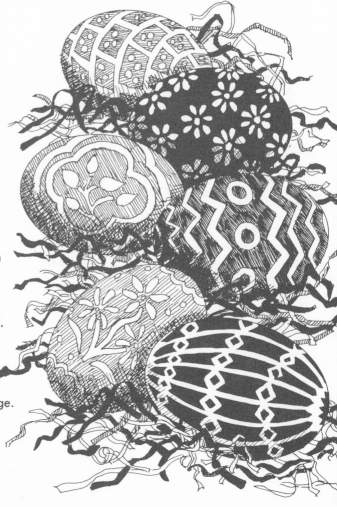

PASTILLAGE

The art of pastillage is modeling objects from sugar paste. Pastillage is elegant; it has the fragile, pastel look of frosting and is permanent if kept away from moisture. Do not pick the baskets up by the handles. If they do break, glue the pieces back together with Elmer's Glue.

Making Sugar Paste

Ingredients: 1½ tsp. unflavored gelatin; ¼ cup cold water; 1 package confectioners sugar; corn starch for the kneading surface.

Sprinkle gelatin into the water and let soften for 5 minutes. Set the bowl in a pan of hot water and heat. Stir occasionally until gelatin is dissolved. Cool slightly.

Combine gelatin with 2 cups sugar in a medium-sized bowl. Stir until completely blended. Gradually add remaining sugar. Using a sifter, sprinkle corn starch onto a pastry board. Knead until the dough is satiny smooth. Wrap in plastic wrap immediately.

Working with the Dough

Always work on a surface on which you have sifted a light dusting of corn starch.

Keep all dough wrapped in plastic except the piece you are using. If the dough dries or cracks while you are working with it, soften with a few drops of water and reknead.

To color the dough, break off a piece—as much as you need—drop food coloring directly on it and knead until it absorbs the moisture.

Making the Baskets

The baskets, minus decorations and handle, each consist of about ⅓ of the dough. Have a glass of water and a brush (a basting brush is fine) handy. Make each basket as follows.

Color ⅓ of the dough as desired. Recover with plastic. Break off a finger-sized piece. Roll it on the cornstarch-sprinkled counter with your hands, just as you would clay. Coil it like a braided rug and brush water sparingly between the coils to make them stick together. Then roll another piece. Attach it to the first by pinching the ends together; coil and brush on water. Roll, pinch together, coil and brush, working quickly until the basket is made. Shape the coils into a round or diamond, forming the floor first and then building up the walls.

Making the Handle

Roll a coil ¼" x 8"-9" long. Roll it flat with a glass. Wet the ends and press the handle in place inside the basket. Keep it propped up while it dries by placing a small box topped with a crumpled piece of tissue paper or wax paper inside the basket. When dry, snake the props out.

Decorations

Pebbles, petals and leaves are all made as if you were modeling clay. Pinch off a bit of dough, color, shape and let dry. Affix to dry baskets with Elmer's Glue. If you are working around a basket and must turn it on its side, wait until the glue attaching one decoration is dry before moving on to the next.

HOW TO MAKE A BIRDFEEDER

These simple practical birdfeeders take a half hour to make, cost less than a dollar.

SQUASH BIRDFEEDER

Cut off part of the side of a squash and scoop out the pulp. Put 2 holes in the top of the squash with a nail and hammer. Use the nail to push a strand of string through each hole. Tie together the ends of string that are inside the squash and tie the other ends of the string to a branch on a tree or bush. Fill the feeder with sunflower seeds or other bird food.

GRAPEFRUIT BIRDFEEDER

Hollow out half a grapefruit, leaving the rind. Put 3 holes in the grapefruit just below the rim by pushing a nail through. Use the nail to push 2" of a long strand of string through each hole and tie just above the rim. Tie the long ends of string together. Attach to a branch on a tree or bush. Fill the grapefruit with water.

PINE CONE BIRDFEEDER

Wind a piece of wire around a large pine cone so the wire is held between the pieces of bark on the cone. Prepare a feed of suet and sunflower seeds: First put the beef suet through a food grinder and then melt it down; let the suet cool, mash the seeds into it and spread it on the cone. If you do not want to use suet, mash the sunflower seeds in peanut butter.

Attach the wire to a branch of a tree or bush.

KITCHEN SPROUTS

Recycle the remains of fruits and vegetables into easy-to-grow, indoor house plants.

PINEAPPLE

Cut off the thick leaves and most of the fruit, leaving only about 2". Set the remaining part in a dish containing water, pebbles and crushed charcoal. In few weeks, when leaves and roots are formed, transplant into a soil-filled pot and place in a sunny spot. To make the plant flower and form edible fruit, place an apple in the pineapple leaves and cover the entire plant with a clear plastic bag for 4 or 5 days. (The apple emits gas fumes that force the pineapple to produce.) When you remove the bag, you will see new leaves on the plant, and shortly thereafter, the first signs of fruit will appear at the bottom of these leaves.

CARROTS & BEETS

Cut off the leaves and bottom of the vegetable, leaving only the top with stubby stems coming out. Place in a dish containing water and a few stones. Do not submerge. When roots and green leaves are formed, transplant to a soil-filled pot.

SWEET POTATO

Select a plump sweet potato. In case the potato has been sprayed with sprout inhibitor, place it in a dark room for several days to break dormancy. Then poke 3 toothpicks into the potato and suspend it in a glass filled with enough water to cover the bottom of the potato. Place the glass in a cool, dark place for two weeks. Then keep it near a sunny window. The potato will grow into a beautiful vine.

ORANGE, LEMON & GRAPEFRUIT

For best results, use the fattest seeds. Plant them in pots containing a layer of small stones on the bottom and a soil mix of 2 parts garden soil, 1 part sand, 1 part peat moss. Water a little each day to keep the soil moist but not wet.

COOKING FIRES

Grill Fire
A shallow depression is edged with parallel rows of rocks. Grill balances between them.

Basic Hot Dog Roast Fire
The ground is cleared and a shallow depression dug. Area is circled with stones and fire built in center. Roast food on sticks.

The One-Pot Fire
A saucepan, frying pan or coffee pot stands on a rock. Sticks circle the rock and as they burn, the rock conducts the heat.

Two Fires for Making Stews and Soups
Two forked sticks are hammered into the ground and a sturdy branch runs between them.

Three sticks are hammered into the ground and tied in triangular fashion with heavy-weight string or cord.

An Instant Cupboard

WINDCHIME

Materials: 18 scallop shells in assorted sizes (several extras in case they break); for the chimes, 6 pieces of string, each 12″ long; for the braided handle, 3 pieces of the same string that was used for the chimes, 3 pieces of string in another color and 3 pieces of narrow ribbon or braid in a third color—9 altogether and each 24″ long; 1 small curtain ring, ½″-1″ in diameter; the inner hoop of a wooden embroidery hoop; thin nail; hammer; Elmer's Glue.

Hammer one hole in each shell: Put the shell on the table (protect the table with heavy cardboard) and hammer the point of the nail through the shell with a sharp tap. Some shells will break, some will resist altogether, but most will come out fine.

Take the 9 pieces of string and ribbon or braid for the handle and divide them into sets of 3—one of each type in a set. Tie each set to the embroidery hoop equidistant from each other. Braid until each set is 12″ long. Tie the braids together in a knot at the 7″ mark—7″ from the hoop. Then braid the braids together. When you come to the end, make a knot and tie the ends to a curtain ring.

Tie the pieces of string for the chimes around the hoop equidistant from each other. Attach 3 shells to each string as follows:

If the size of the shells vary, they should be attached to each string in order of size—largest to smallest. Stiffen the end of the string with glue and slip the string through the hole in the shell.

Push the shell way up the string; then, below the shell, about 5″ from the hoop, tie a double knot in the string. When you hold up the windchime, the knot will keep the shell in place on the string. Slip on a second shell, tie a knot and then a third and tie a knot.

When you have slipped on and secured all the shells, dab glue on all knots to secure them.

HOW TO DO RELIEF PRINTING

Naturally you need a relief before you can do relief printing. So begin by making a collage, combining a variety of materials—this is the relief. Then make a print of it: Roll ink over the relief, cover with rice paper and rub. When you lift the paper, you will see the textures and shapes of the relief printed on it.

Materials: 1 piece of heavy cardboard or mat board, any size, as a ground for the relief; oil-base block printing ink; piece of glass (sharp edges should be taped with masking tape) on which to roll out the ink; 1 soft rubber brayer, 4″ wide (e.g., Speedball #64); an additional soft roller, either a brayer or an inexpensive paint roller about 3″ or 4″ wide, turpentine and rags for cleaning the brayer and glass; soft rice paper or tableau paper, enough for several prints (see step 3 for size); Elmer's Glue; materials for making the relief (see step 1).

1. Collect materials for the relief—anything goes as long as it is fairly flat; bits of lace, rickrack, textured fabric, sequins, spangles, feathers, yarn, string, flowers, grasses, leaves, spices like bay leaf and caraway seeds, toothpicks, matches, steel wool, cardboard cutouts, corrugated paper, wire mesh or screen, aluminum foil, flat hardware like washers, coins and buttons.

Using the glue, make a collage on the cardboard. Let dry for a couple of hours. If the glue is not completely dry, the wet ink will pull the pieces off and onto the brayer.

2. Cut several pieces of rice (or tableau) paper about 6″ wider and 6″ longer than the relief. Set aside until you are ready to print.

3. (Printing the relief) Squeeze about 1″ of ink on the glass. Roll the soft rubber brayer back and forth over the ink until the ink is very tacky and the brayer is evenly coated. Then roll the brayer firmly over 1 section of the relief to cover it with a film of ink. Ink up the brayer again and roll over another section. Continue in this manner until the entire relief is inked.

Lay a piece of rice paper over the inked relief, centering it as best you can. ONCE YOU PUT THE PAPER DOWN, DO NOT MOVE IT OR THE PRINT WILL BE FUZZY. Hold it steady with one hand while you roll your other, clean, brayer firmly over the entire relief. Lift up the paper carefully so it does not smudge. Examine it. Did you apply enough or too much ink to the relief before printing? Did you roll firmly enough over the paper to get a sharp print? Is the design interesting? Make other prints, correcting any miscalculations and experimenting with different colors of ink, if you like. Let the prints dry in a safe place overnight. The prints can be matted or framed.

4. When you are finished, clean the brayer and glass, first with a rag dipped in turpentine; second, with soap and warm water.

HISTORIC RUBBINGS

Look through historic graveyards for gravestones with unusual Early American or
Victorian carvings on them. Or look for low-relief designs cast or carved into buildings
or on signs. Take with you jumbo crayons, masking tape, a dusting brush and paper
(wide, white shelf paper, rice or other thin, sensitive paper). Clean off the surface
with the brush and tape the paper on to cover the design. Color the paper with
the side of the crayon, stroking across in one direction. The carved design will emerge.
When you return home, rub the design with a sock or soft cloth to make it shine.

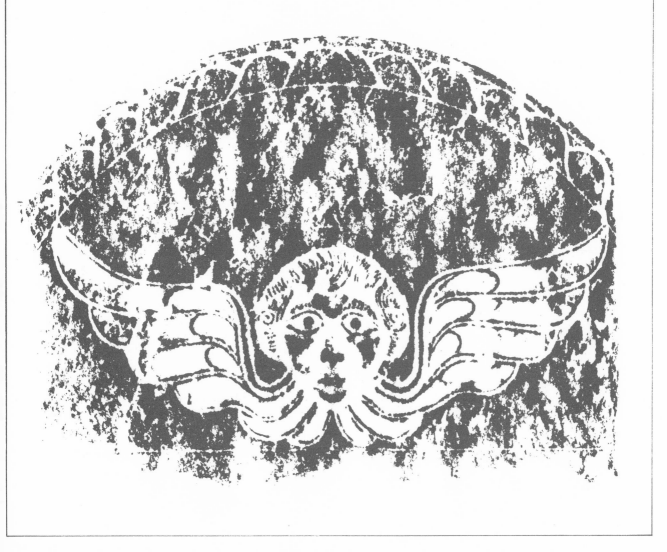

FLYING MACHINE

Materials: 2 boxes (A & B)—one slightly larger than the other; 1 long box (C); extra cardboard boxes for wing and tail pieces; Elmer's Glue; mat knife or single-edge razor blades; strong tape (Mystik or gaffer tape); metal straight edge or metal ruler; large piece of colored paper; enamel or poster paint and brush; decorations (see step 6).

Note: Use the mat knife or single-edge blades to cut the cardboard.

1. Fit boxes A and B together by cutting out as shown. Then make the windshield as shown. Glue boxes together at points of contact at bottom and sides. Tape them securely to hold while the glue dries.

2. Cut slots for wings in box B. Cut wings, put glue on ends and slide into slots.

3. Cut tail pieces. Score and bend as shown. Tape C closed; glue and tape tail pieces to C.

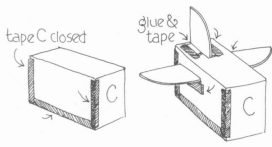

4. Glue and tape C to B.

5. Make a nose cone from a large piece of colored paper: Roll the paper into a cone and glue. Cut tabs in the large end of the cone and glue to A.

6. Paint the airplane. When the paint is dry, decorate with labels from cans, magazine pictures, decals, trading cards like baseball cards, comics, bumper stickers. Tie on balloons and take off!

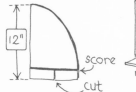

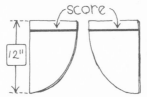

BATHTUB TOYS

INSTANT SHOWER
Thoroughly wash out an old plastic bottle that has a handle. Poke or hammer holes in the bottom with a nail. The child fills it with water and holds it over her head for a homemade shower.

SQUIRT GLOVES
Snip tiny holes in the tips of the fingers of a rubber glove. The child fills the glove with water and squeezes. Presto, a 5-way shot. It is a wise precaution to draw the shower curtain at least partially across the bathtub when this game is being played.

SPONGE MITT
Cut a piece of thin, inexpensive sponge into a mitt shape. It will be easiest to cut the sponge when it's wet. Poke 4 holes in the sponge with a nail. Use the nail again to poke strips of narrow elastic through the holes. Fit the elastic to the child's hand and knot.

SUPPLY BOAT
Poke holes with a nail just below the rims of 4 plastic margarine containers. Tie them together with string. Float the supply boat in the tub and fill it with even smaller bathtub toys.

HOW TO MAKE PLACE MATS

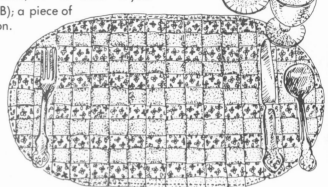

Materials for 4 place mats: cotton or synthetic cotton fabric, 44"–45" wide—2 yds. of 1 color or print (type A) and 2 yds. of another (type B); a piece of paper exactly 13" X 18"; fabric glue; ruler; scissors; iron.

PREPARING THE MATERIALS

1. Make the template: Rule the paper into 1" squares and draw in the rounded corners, using the graph as a guide. Cut the corners along the curved lines.

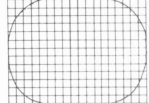

2. Straighten 1 cut edge of each piece of fabric by snipping the selvage close to the corner and tearing straight across. Iron the fabric. Starting at the straightened edge, snip the selvage every 3". Tear the fabric in 3" strips at the snips. You should have at least 23 strips of each fabric. Iron them.

3. Fold each strip lengthwise with right sides together. Sew across 1 short end close to the selvage and then down the length, 1/2" from the ragged edge. Sew 23 strips of A and 21 strips of B. Trim all seam allowances to 1/4".

4. Turn the strips right side out: Push the short stitched end up into itself with a pencil; continue pushing the tube of fabric down over the pencil until the end covered by the pencil emerges; pull the fabric all the way down until it is right side out; then slide the pencil out.

Cut off the stitched short end of all strips as close to the ends as possible. Iron the strips flat, centering the seamline. The sides with the seamline will be on the underside of the mat. Cut the strips into 18" and 13" lengths as shown.

WEAVING EACH MAT

1. Take 18 13" strips, 9 A's, 9 B's; and 13 18" strips, 7 A's, 6 B's. Line up the 18" strips horizontally, alternating A's and B's, keeping all ends even. Lay the 13" strips on top of them vertically, alternating A's and B's and keeping ends even. Keep all strips in a perfect rectangle. Weave the ends over and under on 1 long and 1 short side as shown. Tack together with fabric glue.

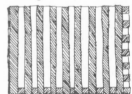

2. Weave the short strips under and over, continually pulling the short and long strips into alignment. Every strip must stay at right angles to every other strip or the mat will come out lopsided. Keep the weaving tight and smooth. When the weaving is completed, use fabric glue to tack down loose ends of the other long and short sides.

3. Now you have a rectangular mat. Lay the oval template over it and with pencil or chalk, draw around the curved corners. Cut off the corners of the mat along the pencil line. Turn under the edge of the mat 1/2" and iron. Topstitch 1/4" from the edge. Iron again.

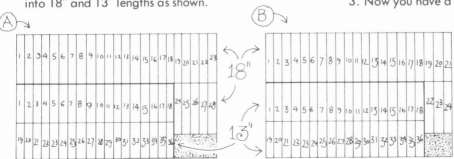

BASKETS, BASKETS, BASKETS

Baskets are a popular item these days. Many of those available are inexpensive; some can be had just for the asking. The types we have in mind are wooden fruit baskets with vertical wooden slats, smaller similar wooden baskets that mushrooms are shipped and sold in, wicker laundry baskets and straw baskets that are imported in all sizes and shapes. With a little ingenuity, you can decorate these simple baskets and put them to use beautifully all over the home—as magazine holders, wastebaskets, containers for office, art or craft supplies, yarn holders, storage bins for children's toys.

WHERE TO GET THEM

Produce and mushroom baskets are either given away or sold at a nominal price by fruit vendors. Wicker and straw baskets are sold at import stores.

HOW TO DECORATE THEM

Paint them in bright colors—at least 3 colors to a basket. Use small jars of enamel paint sold at 5-and-10-cent stores.

Decorate wooden baskets with old-fashioned decals of flowers, fruits, toys, animals. Decals are sold at art supply stores. Apply these decals to painted baskets or apply them to unpainted wood baskets and then paint on a coat of shellac.

Wicker and straw baskets look especially nice with materials woven through them. Some possibilities: grosgrain ribbon, striped ribbon, raffia (a straw often used by crocheters), unusual textured yarn for weaving or knitting, jute and twine. To thread the material easily through the weave of the basket and around the rim, thread it on a yarn needle. Secure the ends of the material with a drop or 2 of glue.

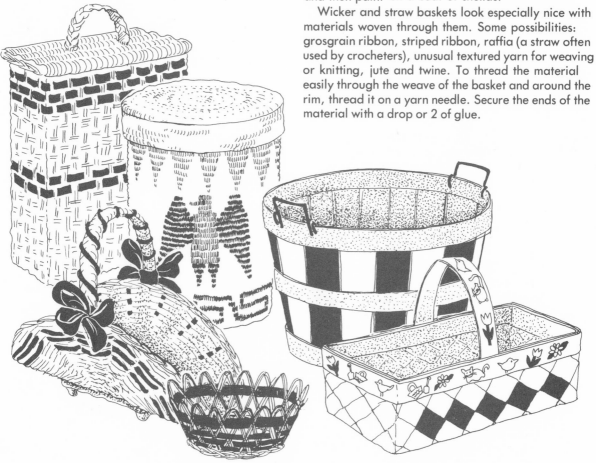

HOW TO MAKE A SEA SHELL NECKLACE

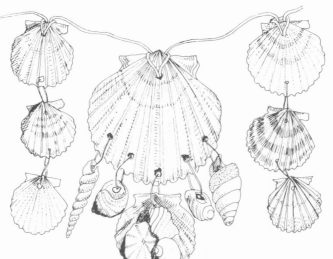

Materials: 1 large scallop shell about 2½" across; 7 medium-size scallop shells, each about 1½" across, and a few extras; at least 7 assorted small shells and a few extras; Elmer's Glue; white string like Speed-Cro-Sheen sold at the 5-and-10; white heavy duty thread; hammer and thin nail.

The large scallop needs 6 holes; 4 of the medium-size scallops need 2 holes and 3 need 1 hole. Select 4 of the assorted small shells to dangle from the large scallop and give them 1 hole each. Make holes in shells like this: Place the shell on a sturdy surface protected by cardboard, place the point of the nail against the shell where you want the hole and send the nail through the shell with a sharp tap of the hammer. A few shells will break—that's why you need some extras—but most will survive intact.

String the large scallop on a piece of string 40" long. Fold the string in half and push the folded end through the hole in the top of the shell. If you have trouble doing this, dab glue on the folded part to stiffen it and then poke it through. Thread both ends of string through the loop and pull tight.

Use this same method to string on 1 scallop shell with 2 holes in it on each side of the large shell. Adjust the space between shells to about 1¾" from hole to hole and pull all loops tight.

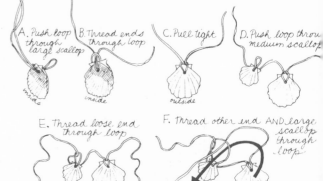

A. Push loop through large scallop

B. Thread ends through loop

C. Pull tight

D. Push loop through medium scallop

E. Thread loose end through loop

F. Thread other end AND large scallop through loop

Tie on the other shells with thread. Cut the ends of thread close to the knots. Glue an assortment of shells inside the center bottom scallop shell and dab bits of glue on all the knots of thread.

Wear the necklace by tying the string around your neck.

KID'S CAR KIT
Next time you take a trip, be prepared.

Take a 6- or 8-bottle soda container. Make it your child's official car kit by labeling it with his name spelled out in adhesive letters. Then fill it up. A few comic books. A fortune teller. A ball of thick yarn or nylon rope: if you cut it into 3 pieces and tie them to something in the car, your child can braid while you drive. Just don't tie them to the door handle. A ball of string to play Jacob's Ladder or Cat's Cradle. A small thermos of apple juice and a straw. A box of animal crackers. A few large felt-tipped markers. Large post cards and stamps—it's time Grandma received a note or a hand-drawn picture post card. A scorecard for car games like Out-of-State or Ghost or to use as a log book—what sights did you see on the road?

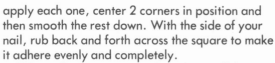

GAME BOARDS

CHESS

This plexiglass chess board is astonishingly easy to make. The squares are cut from a sheet of pressure-sensitive film that is sold at art supply stores in a variety of colors under such brand names as Zipatone, Letratone and Pantone. When you buy the film, it is on a waxed backing sheet. To use it, cut the size square you need, peel it off the backing (just as you peel a bumpersticker off its backing) and put the film in place. The back of the film is adhesive—it will immediately stick to the surface you press it on. The film makes an almost flat surface and the translucent color contrasts beautifully with the transparency of the plexiglass.

Materials: 1 piece of clear plexiglass, 17" square, ¼" thick (sold at plastics suppliers); 2 sheets of Zipatone, Letratone or Pantone (or the equivalent) in a bright dark color; 1 single-edge razor blade; steel ruler; felt tip pen; pencil.

Make all markings on the plexiglass with a felt tip pen. Place the plexiglass on a light surface and mark off a 1½" border around the edge. Then divide the center area into 1¾" squares—8 across and 8 down. Put an X on every other square.

With a pencil, mark off the Zipatone (or the equivalent) into 1¾" squares. Cut out the squares with a razor. You don't need to apply much pressure on the razor since it is necessary to cut only through the film, not through the waxed backing.

Peel off each square and put it on the plexiglass on each square not marked with an X. When you apply each one, center 2 corners in position and then smooth the rest down. With the side of your nail, rub back and forth across the square to make it adhere evenly and completely.

When all squares are in place, wipe off the X's and other pen markings with a damp cloth or sponge.

To use the board, place it squares side down. You will see the colored squares clearly through the transparent plexiglass and the surface for the game will be level and smooth.

BACKGAMMON

A decoupage technique transforms an inexpensive backgammon board into a fancy table model.

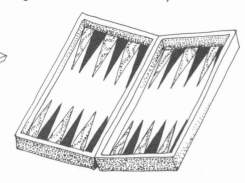

Materials: 1 plastic backgammon board; decoupage cut-outs from fancy paper, i.e. marbleized paper, glossy paper like flint paper, solid color wrapping paper; Krylon Spray; Elmer's Glue; paint brush; paper cup; sponge.

Spray the board with Krylon. Dilute glue in a paper cup with several drops of water. Brush glue on the cut-outs and arrange in collages that completely cover but do not exceed the edges of each triangle on the board. Wipe off excess glue with a damp sponge as you work. Let dry overnight.

Apply 3 layers of Krylon a day for several days until the surface is glossy and level. Always let the coat of spray dry completely before applying another one.

TENNIS TOTE

Materials: 1 piece of fabric, 30" x 7", and 2 circles of fabric, 10" in diameter (use light canvas, duck, sail cloth, corduroy, denim or burlap); a 16" zipper; 4 pieces of 1½"-wide gros grain ribbon, each 9" long; heavy duty thread to match the fabric; a #18 needle and zipper foot for the sewing machine.

1. (Preparing the handles) Pin the ribbons together in pairs. Sew the short ends ½" from the edges. Turn inside out and iron. Sew around the perimeter about 1/8" from the edge.

2. Turn under the short ends of the main piece ½" and iron to make a crease.

3. With pencil, mark the placement of each handle on the fabric—one will be attached to the main piece and the other to one of the circles. Notice in the drawing that although each handle is 8" long, it will cover a space only 7½" long. This is so that you can use the handle when the tote is finished and packed. Pin each handle in place with the excess ribbon pushed to the center. Insert the #18 needle in the sewing machine and sew each handle to the fabric with an X-shape at each end.

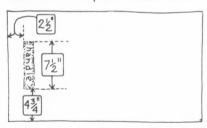

4. Pin the closed zipper to the turned-under edge of the fabric as shown. Attach the zipper foot to the sewing machine with the foot to the left of the needle. Sew the zipper, from bottom to top, to the fabric about 1/16" from the fold.

Bring the other turned-under edge of the main piece around and pin to the closed zipper. Move the zipper foot to the right of the needle and sew again, close to the fold, from the bottom of the zipper to the top. The fabric forms a tube.

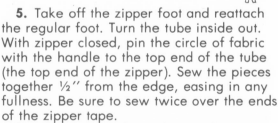

5. Take off the zipper foot and reattach the regular foot. Turn the tube inside out. With zipper closed, pin the circle of fabric with the handle to the top end of the tube (the top end of the zipper). Sew the pieces together ½" from the edge, easing in any fullness. Be sure to sew twice over the ends of the zipper tape.

Reach into the tube and unzip the zipper. Leaving the tube inside out, pin the other circle of fabric in place. Sew the pieces together ½" from the edge, easing in fullness and sewing twice over the ends of the zipper tape. Turn the tote right side out.

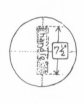

BANGLES, SHELLS & BEADS

Delicate shell-studded bracelets are made by covering bangles with a design of tiny shell flowers. Order the shells through the mail from a craft supply house, or buy them at a craft and hobby store.

Materials: inexpensive plastic or wood bangle bracelets (wide) sold at 5-and-10's; tiny shells; seed beads; Elmer's Glue; tweezer; toothpicks.

Begin by pouring some glue on a piece of paper. With the tweezers or your fingers, whichever is easier, dip the shells in glue and arrange them in a design on the bangle. The shells may slip around a bit, but the glue dries fairly quickly. Then using the toothpick as an applicator, apply dots of glue to the shells and put the seed beads in position.

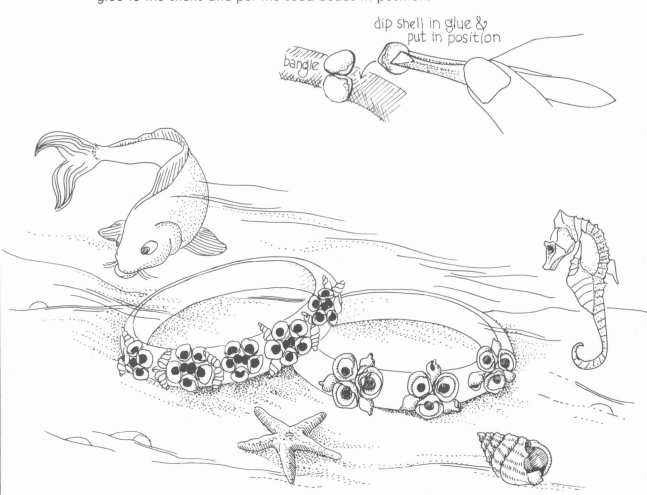

dip shell in glue &
put in position

bangle

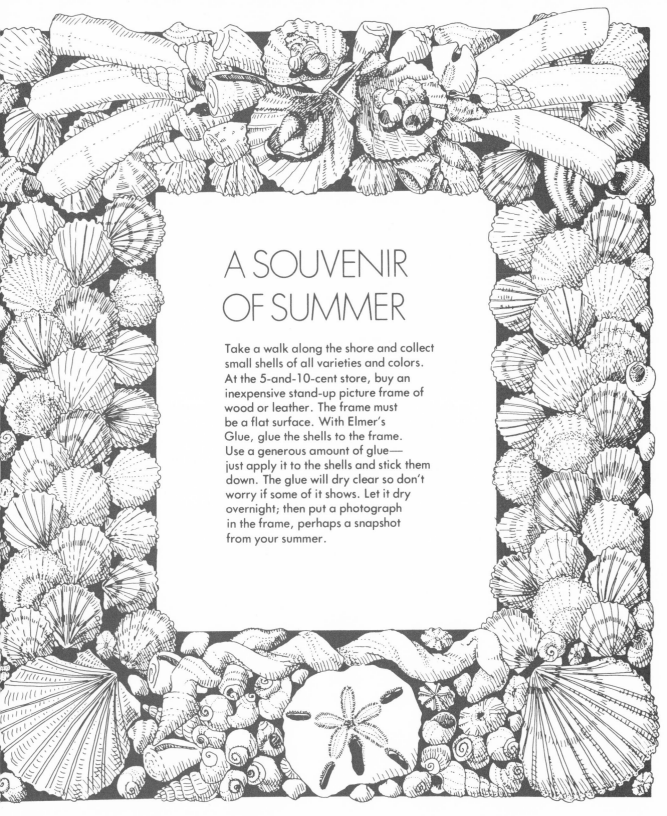

A SOUVENIR OF SUMMER

Take a walk along the shore and collect small shells of all varieties and colors. At the 5-and-10-cent store, buy an inexpensive stand-up picture frame of wood or leather. The frame must be a flat surface. With Elmer's Glue, glue the shells to the frame. Use a generous amount of glue— just apply it to the shells and stick them down. The glue will dry clear so don't worry if some of it shows. Let it dry overnight; then put a photograph in the frame, perhaps a snapshot from your summer.

SANDCAST CANDLES

Materials: sand; 1 flowerpot for each candle; crayons (optional); household paraffin (approximately ¼ lb. for each candle); candle wick; pencil; empty can with label removed; small pebbles.

Break up the wax and put pieces in the empty can. Fill a small pot ⅓ full of water, put the can in the pot and the pot on the stove. Turn on the burner to a low heat. If you want colored candles, put a piece of crayon in the melting wax. While the wax melts, prepare the candle mold.

Fill the flowerpot with <u>moist</u> sand. Dig out the candle shape—use your hand or press an object into the sand like a small rubber ball or a small can. Important: You are making the candle upside down—the sand at the bottom of the mold shapes the top of the candle. To make the candles like strange sea creatures, make large or small holes in the sand jutting out from the basic candle shape: push out the holes with your fingers or poke them with a pencil or stick.

When the mold is finished, tie a pebble to the end of a strand of wick and embed the pebble in the sand at the bottom of the mold as shown. Wind the other end of the wick around the pencil and balance on top of the flowerpot. Be sure the wick is straight.

Pour the liquid wax into the mold carefully. In a few minutes the wax will sink a bit—pour more in to level what will be the bottom of the candle. Let the wax dry completely.

To unmold, turn the flowerpot upside down. All the sand will come out in a hunk in your hand as it does when you repot a plant. Carefully remove the candle. Brush off as much sand as possible. Let dry and brush off again. A very thin coating of sand should remain on the candle surface.

LEAF PRINT STATIONERY

Five-and-tens, large drugstores and stationery stores all sell folded notepaper and inexpensive writing pads of colored paper, absolutely plain, with packages of envelopes to match. Buy a set either in assorted colors or in one color—they will be the basis of your personalized stationery.

Collect an assortment of fresh, small leaves, and always experiment with them on scrap paper before you make prints on stationery.

POSITIVE PRINTS—THE STAMP PAD TECHNIQUE

Place a leaf on a stamp pad and cover it with a piece of plastic wrap. Rub over the leaf and plastic wrap gently to ink up the leaf. Lift the plastic and remove the leaf with tweezers. Place the leaf, ink side down, in position on a piece of stationery or folded notepaper and cover it with a small piece of scrap paper. Gently rub to print the leaf.

Make identical prints on envelopes to match.

NEGATIVE PRINTS—THE SPATTER TECHNIQUE

Put a few drops of a pretty color of India Ink or liquid concentrated watercolors in a shallow container. Dilute with a tablespoon or 2 of water, depending on how pale or dark you want the color. Put 1 or more leaves in position on the paper and weigh them down with a few coins. Dip an old toothbrush into the diluted color and shake off the excess drops. Holding the toothbrush about 1½" from the paper with the bristles pointing down, flick your finger tips briskly over the bristles. Repeat this technique using 1 to five colors until the paper is delicately sprinkled. Carefully remove the leaves. Spatter envelopes to match.

HOW TO MAKE & USE A FLOWER PRESS

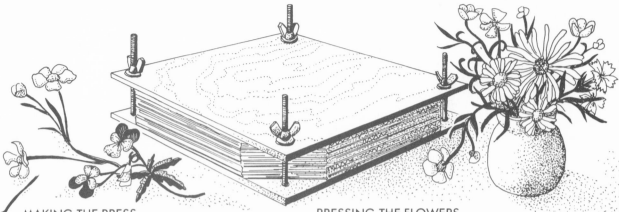

MAKING THE PRESS

Materials: 2 pieces of ¼" plywood, 12" square, with a hole drilled 1" from each corner; 4 3" screws (#10-24) with wing nuts to fit; 8 washers that fit over the screws; 8 pieces of corrugated cardboard, 12" square, with the corners cut off; 14 sheets of blotting paper, 12" square, with the corners cut off.

Put the press together like a Dagwood sandwich. First lay down a piece of plywood; then add 1 piece of cardboard, then 2 blotters. Continue alternating 1 piece of cardboard with 2 sheets of blotting paper ending with cardboard; top the stack off with the other piece of plywood. After the flowers are placed between the sheets of blotting paper, insert the screws, washers, and nuts to fasten the corners as shown. Turn the nuts to tighten the sandwich.

If you want to decorate the press, stain or shellac the wood or apply a decoupage design.

PRESSING THE FLOWERS

The flowers must be very fresh—take the press with you when you go collecting or take a jar of water to hold the cut flowers. Select flowers that are not too thick at the center or stem because the blotting paper must touch all parts of the flower. Suggested kinds: buttercups, ferns, grasses, pansies, violets, daisies (if the centers are not thick), roses (press the petals separately). Open the press and spread the flowers out carefully on 7 of the sheets of blotting paper. The flowers should not touch each other and should be spread all over the paper, not just at the center. It helps to use tweezers. Top each flower-covered blotter with 1 of the 7 remaining blotters. Restack the pieces of the press and tighten the nuts. Important: Leave the flowers to dry in the press at least 4 weeks, possibly as long as 6. Check after 2 and 3 weeks—you may have to change the sheets of blotting paper if they become saturated. Keep the finished dried flowers away from dampness.

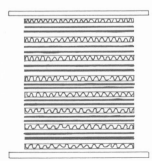

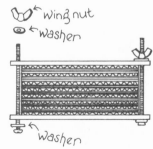

wing nut

washer

washer

HOW TO DRY FLOWERS & HERBS

Always work with flowers and herbs when they are dry (not wet from dew or rain), fresh and perfect-looking.

AIR DRYING

For stalk-type, seed pod, straw-like and grassy flowers and herbs.
Examples—milkweed, everlasting, cockscomb, grains, heather, goldenrod, tarragon, thyme and basil.

Group a few in a bundle, tie tightly with a string or rubber band and hang upside down from a nail or hanger in a place where the air will circulate around them. Let them dry 7-10 days.

When they are dried, arrange the flowers and herbs in a vase or shred the herbs into small pieces, store them in closed jars and use for cooking.

CORNMEAL AND BORAX

For delicate flowers. Examples—roses, chrysanthemums, peonies, lilies, daisies, asters, zinnias, snapdragons, wildflowers.

Mix together 4 cups yellow cornmeal, 4 cups powdered borax and 6 tablespoons of salt (not iodized.) Spread ½ layer of the mixture in the bottom of a large cardboard box lined with wax paper.

Remove most of the leaves from the stems of the flowers. Space the flowers about 4" apart in the box as follows: hold each flower upside down and gently push it into the mixture. Holding the stem, use a tablespoon to sprinkle the mixture in and about the flower so its head is completely covered. Leave for 10 days.

Take the flowers out of the mixture and shake them lightly. If the stems are wobbly or won't support the heads of the flowers, wire the stems to pipe cleaners or twigs. Arrange them in a pretty clay flower pot, crock, basket or vase. (To hold flowers in place in the container, put sand or a flower holder in the bottom and push the stems into it.)

marshpink

black-eyed susan

twin-leaved coneflower

aster

wild geranium

musk mallow

GREETING CARDS

For birthdays, anniversaries, holidays, announcements & party invitations

Cut construction paper of assorted colors into ½" squares. Glue them in a design to another piece of construction paper, 4½" square. Write your message on the back. Make a construction paper envelope to match.

11"

7½"

glue

fold

PARTY FAVORS

SURPRISE PACKAGE

Stuff toilet paper rolls with hard candies. Roll each of them in a rectangle of crepe paper. Hold the crepe paper in place with a sticker, tie off with yarn and fringe the ends.

 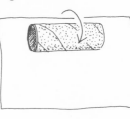 

PLACE CARDS

Cut rectangles of white card stock or use the blank side of index cards. Fold in half. Decorate the front with an assortment of shells, a feather, a ribbon bow or a paper flower. Write a guest's name on each.

JEAN APPLIQUÉS

Cut iron-on patches into pretty shapes—stars, hearts, diamonds, circles. Give 1 to each child with the initial of her first name embroidered on it.

FORTUNE TELLER Fold a piece of colored paper, 8″ square, as shown.

Write the name of a color on each outside square. Write a number on each inside triangle. Open up completely and write a fortune on each triangle. Refold and shape the fortune teller into a cone so it can be opened using the thumb and forefinger of each hand.

The fortune teller game works like this. A child picks a color. The reader spells the color aloud, opening the fortune teller one way and then the other, alternating with letters. On the last letter, the child looks in and picks a number. The reader looks under the number and reads the fortune.

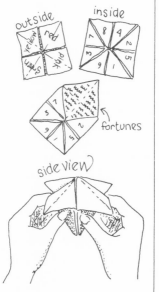

① Fold corners in
② Turn over & fold corners in again
③ Bring corners in together
④ Pull lower corners out

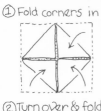

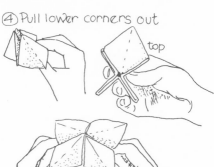

MINIATURE GARDENS

For miniature gardens, you need miniature containers, preferably in natural materials—clam shells, mussel shells, small wooden boxes like the kind brie and camembert cheese come in, small ceramic saucers, rocks with naturally-eroded pockets; driftwood with natural pockets, clay saucers from flower pots.

FRESH FLOWER GARDEN

Pick small flowers—tiny wildflowers, pansies, grape hyacinths, johnny jump-ups, sweet peas, violets. Fill the container with a piece of Oasis. (Oasis is a spongy material that retains moisture and serves as a flower-holder at the same time. Buy it at any florist.) Pour water on the Oasis until it will not absorb any more. Insert the flower stems into the Oasis. If you have trouble poking the stems in, pave the way with a toothpick.

CACTUS GARDEN

Buy a tiny cactus. Put a drop of Elmer's Glue in the bottom of the container. Place the cactus on it. Fill the container with sand, tiny pebbles and a bit of sphagnum moss. Water and place in a sunny spot.

GARDEN OF SUCCULENT PLANTS

Buy a tiny succulent plant—sedums, sempervivums, kalanchoes—or use a cutting from a larger one. Fill the container with sphagnum moss. Put the plant into the moss. Water and put in a cool, light place.

HOW TO MAKE A TERRARIUM

The container for the terrarium can be any glass or clear plastic container with a top—a large jug, mason jar, vase, aquarium, bowl, glass, candy or cookie jar, plastic box. In a pinch, use plastic wrap for a top.

You will need a spoon to help with the planting and perhaps a pair of tongs. If the container has a narrow neck, attach the spoon to a stick with a rubber band.

Cover the bottom of the container with about 2" of fine gravel. On top of that put a very thin layer of sphagnum moss and then a thin layer of activated charcoal. Add the soil (sterilized potting soil mixed with sand and peat moss).

Dig out areas of the soil with the spoon and carefully lower small plants into the scooped-out areas. You may want to use the tongs to hold the plants when you lower them. Good plants to use: ferns, mosses, baby tears, small-leaf begonias, ardisia or baby palms. Put in a little more soil he and there to be sure all roots are covered. Decorate, if you like, with pebbles, rocks, shells, pieces of wood and other natural objects.

Spray lightly with a fine mister and cover the t Put the terrarium in a window where it will get lig but not direct sunlight.

HOW TO MAKE TISSUE PAPER FLOWERS

Each flower is made of a stack of tissue paper disks, pinched at the center with wire and wired to a pipecleaner. The wire is concealed with a strip of tissue paper. As a final touch, the tops of the petals are dipped in diluted food coloring, which is absorbed by the tissue, blending and contrasting with its color.

Materials: Assorted colors of tissue paper; needle; thin wire (buy it on a spool at the 5-and-10-cent store); pipecleaners; Elmer's Glue; food coloring.

DIRECTIONS FOR EACH FLOWER

1. Cut out 10 tissue paper circles, each 4" in diameter. It is easiest to cut them 5 at a time by stacking up squares of tissue. Then fold the circles, several at once, into quarters and cut the outer edge into petal shapes.

2. Unfold, flatten the circles and stack them up. With a needle, puncture 2 holes—¼" apart—through the center. Cut a 10" length of wire and thread it through the holes, pulling the ends even. Pinch the tissue paper flower up, away from the wire.

3. Place a pipecleaner next to the base of the flower. Wind the wire tightly around the pipecleaner to bind it and the base of the flower together. Continue winding the wire around the pipecleaner for ½" or so.

4. Smear glue around the base of the flower and on the wire. Wind a narrow strip of tissue paper around the gluey part to conceal the wire. Add more glue and tissue if necessary.

5. Open the tissue paper petals and spread them carefully. Fill a small dish with a mixture of several drops of food coloring and several drops of water. Dip just the tips of the petals into this solution; don't dip the outermost 2 layers of petals at all. Let them dry.

IDEAS

■ Stack 8 tissue circles of 1 color and top them with 2 of another color. ■ Stack a rainbow of colors.

■ Snip a fringe in the top 2 or 3 circles of tissue. ■ Make the flowers very large or very small.

HOW TO MAKE FABRIC FLOWERS

Make a dozen of these flowers, using an assortment of fabrics, and arrange them in a pretty crock, jar or vase.

Materials: a spool of #36 or #34 wire (sometimes called lacing wire for beaded flowers); scraps of fabric (solids, calico, small cotton prints); scraps of green felt; green yarn; Elmer's Glue; small or medium size ball fringe; ruler; pinking shears.

THE PETALS

Cut a piece of wire 10" long. Bend at the 8" point, shape to form a loop and twist. Place the wire petal on a double thickness of fabric (right sides facing) and draw around the loop, about ¼" away from it. Cut the fabric along the line with pinking shears. Put glue on the loop and sandwich it between the pieces of fabric, this time with wrong sides facing. Let dry. Repeat 5 more times to have 6 petals.

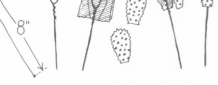

THE LEAVES

Cut a piece of wire 8" long. Bend at the 6" point, shape and twist to form a loop and then flatten the loop. Cut a felt leaf to fit the wire. Put glue on the wire loop and apply the felt leaf to one side of it. Let dry. Repeat once more to have 2 leaves.

THE FLOWER

Stack the petals on top of each other and twist all the stems together. Put glue on the wire stem and wind on green yarn for about ¾". Add a leaf by twisting its stem onto the main stem and continue wrapping the yarn for another ¾". Add another leaf and continue wrapping to the bottom of the stem. Open the petals and shape nicely. Open the leaves out. Glue 3 small or 1 medium size pompom cut from the ball fringe to the center of the flower.

THE BASICS OF PATCHWORK

Patchwork is piecework. Small pieces of fabric are sewn together into larger, more beautiful pieces of fabric. Some patchwork designs consist of blocks of patchwork patterns sewn together; other designs consist of many identical small pieces sewn into a large geometric pattern. Patchwork is used to make quilts, bedspreads, pillows, clothes, stuffed animals, curtains and other household furnishings.

1. Select a patchwork pattern. Draw an overall plan of how your chosen pattern will adapt to the item you want to make. Now you can ascertain exactly how many pieces of each part of the pattern is required.

2. Draw the pattern precisely on the lightweight cardboard or on graph paper glued to cardboard. Number the pieces if you are working with a block design. Cut them out. These cardboard pieces are called templates.

3. Work out a complete color scheme and buy the fabric. All fabric for the patchwork must be the same weight. For example, you might work in cotton and use gingham, plaid, prints and solids. Or you might work in a lush combination of velvet, heavy satin and brocade. Prepare the fabric by washing it (if washable), ironing it and hanging it up on skirt hangers so it won't wrinkle again.

4. Cut the pieces for the patchwork. Each piece is cut as follows: Place the template wrong side up on the wrong side of the fabric; keep the template parallel to either grain of the fabric and draw around it with pencil without stretching the fabric; cut the fabric ¼" outside the pencil line.

5. When you have cut out all the pieces required, sew them together: With right sides facing, sew adjoining pieces together with a short running stitch; sew by hand or machine. You may find it helpful to pin the pieces together first. Follow the pencil lines exactly when sewing.

■ If you are working with a block design, sew the pieces first into blocks. Sew blocks together into rows and then sew rows together.

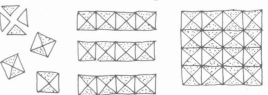

■ If you are working with a large geometric pattern that falls into natural divisions though not into blocks, sew them together first in that way. Then sew the divisions together.

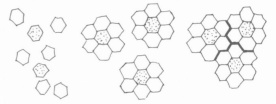

■ If you are working with a large geometric pattern that does not break up naturally, start in the middle and work out.

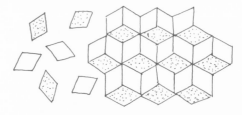

As you complete blocks or sections of patchwork, iron the patchwork on the wrong side, pressing all seam allowances in one direction. Do not press seams open. If you are working with curved pieces of fabric, clip or notch seam allowances after sewing.

THREE PATCHWORK PATTERNS

OHIO STAR
Ohio Star, sometimes called Variable Star, is a simple 9-patch design. Only 2 templates are necessary—a square and a triangle. To determine the exact size of these 2 pieces, draw the whole block.

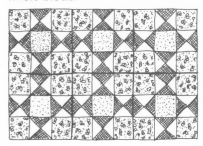 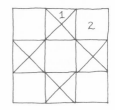

GRANDMOTHER'S FLOWER GARDEN
Grandmother's Flower Garden is an over-all patchwork pattern. It requires one hexagonal template.

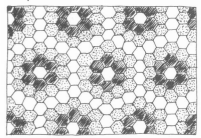 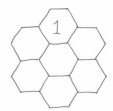

TWIN SISTERS
Twin Sisters is a bold, arresting pattern of repeating blocks. To determine the size of the 2 templates, draw the whole block first.

 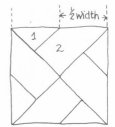 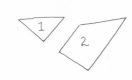

THE FANCIFUL LAMPSHADE

A collage of fabric flowers and a fancy fringe transforms a lamp with an old cloth shade into a Victorian extravaganza.

Buy a half yard of sheer fabric with floral motifs in it. Cut out the individual motifs with pinking shears. Dilute Elmer's Glue in a cup with several drops of water. Glue each motif to the shade: Using a small paint brush, paint a small amount of glue on the shade where the motif will go; center the motif over the glue and apply more glue, working out slowly and carefully—first by putting glue on the shade under the motif and finally on the very edges of the motif. Press down firmly while gluing. Cover the shade with motifs until it is as dense as you like. With undiluted glue, add a border of store-bought silky fringe to the lower edge of the shade. If you like, decorate the top of the fringe and the top edge of the shade with a pretty velvet or embroidered ribbon.

KITCHEN CORNER SPICE SHELVES

Make the shelves out of ¼"
plywood. Cut 3 quadrant-shaped
shelves of the following radii:
6", 9", 12". Have the lumber yard
cut them, ask a friend with a jigsaw
or do it yourself with a coping saw.
Saw or have the lumber yard saw 6
1-by-1 ledger strips (1-by-1 is a
lumber yard term—the actual
measurement, if you take it with
your ruler, is ¾" X ¾"), 2 for each
shelf, of the following lengths: 2
pieces 5" long, 2 8" long, 2 11"
long.

Assemble around you the lumber,
nails, hammer and Elmer's Glue.
Mark the wall where you want each
shelf to go. Glue and nail the ledger
strips to the wall as shown. Glue and
nail the shelves to the ledger strips.
Paint the shelves.

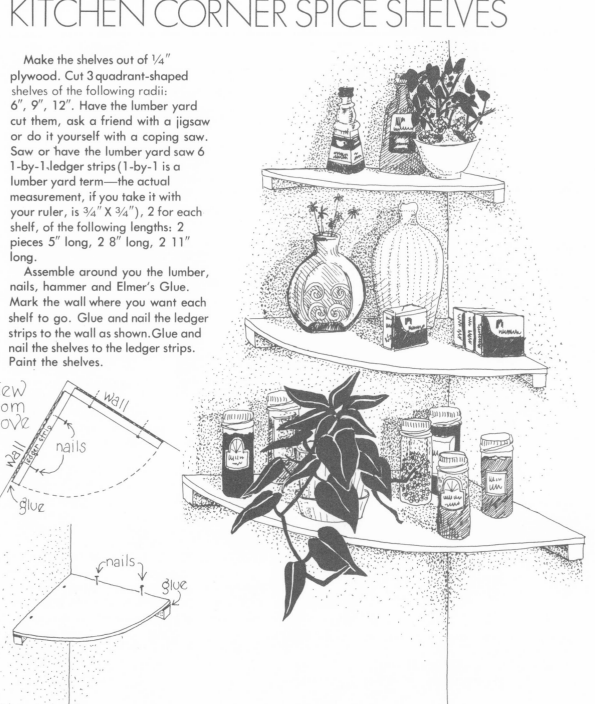

View
from
above

wall

nails

wall

ledger strip

glue

nails

glue

SELLING YOUR CRAFTS

There are all sorts of ways to, if not turn a profit, at least support your habit, from street peddling to opening your own store; but if you are new to the world of marketing, the best ways to begin selling are by organizing your own show and sale, participating in a crafts fair, or selling to small stores like boutiques or gift shops.

ORGANIZING YOUR OWN SHOW & SALE

The advantage to this approach is that the entire profit from the sale of your work goes to you.

Get together with several other craftspersons. Then rent a small exhibit space or, better yet because it will cost nothing, convert a participant's large living room or entire downstairs into an exhibit space. This should not be too inconvenient because the show should last only a day or weekend. A very good time to have the show is early December. People are always looking for presents at that time.

Send out invitations to all your friends and acquaintances. If all the craftspeople participating do this, a large number of people will be reached.

Display the work attractively and mark each one clearly with the price and artist's name. When an object is sold, the cashier can record who made it and how much it cost. Afterward, when you are dividing up the money, you will have no problem apportioning it according to sales volume.

CRAFTS FAIRS

To participate in a craft fair, you pay a registration fee and/or a percentage of money earned in the sale, from 10% to 30%, to the sponsoring organization.

Sometimes you must submit slides of your work and be accepted in order to participate. This screening process insures that a high quality of craft work is exhibited.

Fairs are usually sponsored by guilds or associations of craftspersons, workshops, museums or other art institutions. There are several ways to find out about them. Talk to fellow craftspeople. Call a local museum or gallery that exhibits crafts or folk art. Join a state crafts association to receive their newsletter, which generally keeps its members informed of forthcoming fairs. Subscribe to crafts magazines like Craft Horizons (22 West 55th St., New York, N.Y. 10019).

When you attend a fair, which might be held indoors or outdoors in a meadow or picnic grounds, bring a display table or board with you and arrange your work attractively on it. Half the battle is attracting the shoppers to your display. Also bring a chair—your feet might get tired. Determine your prices beforehand so you don't get put on the spot and regret it later.

SMALL STORES

Boutiques, gift and novelty stores will either buy your work outright or take it on consignment. If they buy outright, you make a profit regardless of whether it sells. However, they will mark up the items 100% and you may have to sell them at a lower price than you would ordinarily like. If they take your work on consignment, they pay only when and if an item sells; however, you earn a higher percentage of the retail price, from 60% to 75%.

Call the store before you go there and speak to the buyer. Say who you are, what you make and ask for a convenient time to show your work.

When you go to the store, have your work packed so you can show it easily, neatly and attractively. The buyer will probably not have time to waste, so your display and negotiations should be efficient: come prepared with prices, delivery date and other information like alternative color combinations for objects shown. If the store buys outright, be sure to include a bill when you deliver the goods. Call the buyer in a week or two to see if your work is selling. If it is, she may want more.

THREE LITTLE BOXES

Materials: 4-ply Bristol board; Elmer's Glue; metal ruler; single-edge razor blades, X-acto knife or mat knife and blades; paper clips; right-angle triangle; a heavy cardboard cutting surface.

> **How To "Score:"** Along the indicated lines make a shallow cut, just breaking the surface of the paper, but not cutting through. Use a mat knife, X-acto or single-edge razor blade. The boards will then fold easily along the scored lines.

Draw the shapes for each box and its cover on the Bristol board. Measure very carefully, using the patterns as guides. Notice that each cover is slightly larger than its box. Cut out each piece with a mat knife, X-acto or single-edge blade, using the metal ruler to guide you. Score the heavy lines as indicated and fold on the scored lines.

Glue the tabs inside each box and cover, and clip while the glue is drying. When dry, remove the clips.

Decorate the boxes. Decoupage would make an especially nice decoration, but there are other possibilities: sequins, ribbon, marbleized paper, gummed stickers, designs drawn with felt-tip markers, paper mosaic or spatter prints.

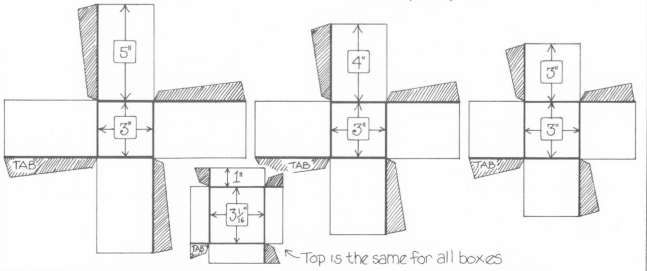

← Top is the same for all boxes

THE BASICS OF APPLIQUÉ

Appliqué, a traditional American sewing craft, involves cutting pretty shapes out of fabric—often images such as hearts, birds, flowers, leaves or geometric shapes—and sewing them in a design to make a quilt or wallhanging, or decorate a piece of clothing, a tablecloth or other household item.

THE BASIC SEWING TECHNIQUE

Draw the shape of the appliqué on a pretty piece of fabric. Cut out the shape an eyeballed ¼" to ½" outside the line. Clip or notch curved edges, clip points and corners of the appliqué. Turn under the edges to the pencil line, baste or tack them down with fabric glue. Iron. Place the appliqué in position on the quilt, clothing or whatever and sew it down by hand with a neat overhand stitch or by machine.

A SPEEDIER IRON-ON TECHNIQUE

Use a fabric for the appliqué with definite motifs in it like flower bouquets, boats, geometric prints or animals. Cut roughly around the motif with pinking shears. Pin the motif to bonding adhesive (a web-like fabric of spun glue, available at any fabric shop or department store —Stitch Witchery is one of the best brands) and cut closely around the motif with pinking shears, cutting the fabric and bonding adhesive at the same time. Put the quilt, clothing or whatever on an ironing board and place the appliqué and bonding adhesive in position on it. Heat baste the appliqué to the material by ironing here and there so the appliqué, bonding adhesive and material stick together lightly. Then remove the pins that hold the appliqué and bonding adhesive together. Iron the appliqué down firmly according to the manufacturer's instructions on the bonding material package.

draw   cut out   clip & notch
notch
clipcorner
notch
clip

turn under & sew

cut out roughly•pin to adhesive & cut closely

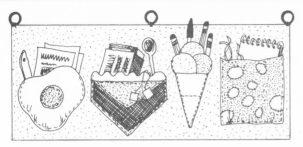

KITCHEN CATCH-ALL

Hang this handy storage unit on the wall or on the side of a cupboard and store in it all the small items that tend to get lost in the shuffle, such as can openers, matches, wire twisters to close plastic bags, toothpicks, dry mix packages like salad dressings, packets of tea, cookie cutters, egg slicers, nutmeg graters, pencils, shopping list.

Materials: scraps of fabric for the pockets and appliqués; 1 rectangle of fabric in heavy cotton or light-weight corduroy, 10¾" x 25" (for a horizontal hanging) or 9" x 32" (a vertical hanging); 3 plastic rings (horizontal) or 2 plastic rings (vertical); needle, thread, pins, sewing machine; paper, tracing paper, pencil, ruler.

Roughly the work goes like this. First you make the basic pockets. Then make and sew on the appliqué detailing like the yolk of the egg and the holes in the cheese. Finally sew the completed pockets to the backing material.

Enlarge the graphs to the sizes indicated. Draw the egg, pie, ice cream cone and Swiss cheese square by square. The heavy lines indicate the basic pockets that will be sewed to the rectangular backing piece. The numbered areas are the appliqués—trace them on tracing paper after you have enlarged the drawing on a graph.

Cut out all the pieces along the outline—the basic pockets out of the graph and the appliqués out of the tracing paper. Draw around these paper patterns on fabric. Using instructions in the Basics of Appliqué (basic sewing technique), make the pockets up to the point at which you would sew them. Then make all the appliqués and fasten them to the pockets using either the basic sewing or iron-on technique.

Gather the lower turned-under edges of the egg, pie and Swiss cheese pockets ½" to ¾". Keeping all edges turned under, sew ⅛" from the edges of all pockets, including the cone. Pull out any basting stitches.

Turn under the edges of the backing piece ½" and sew it ¼" from the edge. Pin all pockets to it, spacing them evenly. Note: When you pin the cone, bring in the side edges a bit to make it gap slightly at the top. This will allow the pocket to be filled without buckling. Sew all the pockets to the rectangle, sewing over the previous sewing. Also sew across the cone horizontally 3" up from the point. Sew plastic rings to the top edges of the backing. Hang on nails or hooks on your wall.

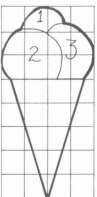

1 box = 1 square inch

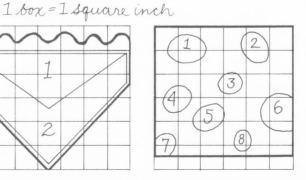

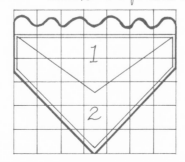

THE RHYTHM SECTION

Keep time to the music with these simple wood and papier maché instruments.

MARACA

Materials: 1 butternut squash with a fairly straight, tapering neck—the very tip of the neck <u>must</u> be narrower than the rest of the neck; Vaseline; ingredients for papier maché (flour, water, and newspaper); a glass; a handful of dried beans, popcorn kernels or tiny pebbles; 1 single-edged razor blade; poster paints and clear lacquer or acrylic paints; paintbrushes.

Make a glue of ½ cup flour and water added slowly until the mixture is smooth and the consistency of thin, not runny, pancake batter. Tear strips of newspaper into 1″ squares and smaller scraps. Smear the squash with a thin coat of Vaseline. Starting from the wide end, cover the squash with papier maché: Hold the squash by the neck in 1 hand and dip scraps of newspaper into the glue with the other hand; apply them to the squash. Cover the squash with 1 layer of papier maché, overlapping the scraps. Rest the wide end of the squash in the glass while you cover it with a second layer. Rest it in the glass overnight to dry.

The next day, use the razor blade to slit the layers of papier maché at the widest point of the squash. Be sure to slit all the way through the paper to the squash. Twist apart the 2 sections in opposite directions; they should come apart with little effort. Remove the squash. If the paper breaks, repair it with new scraps of papier maché.

Put a handful of beans into the hollow top part and rest the hollow neck part over it, matching up the 2 parts by the printing on the paper. Patch the parts together with fresh papier maché. Then add several more layers of papier maché. Let it dry thoroughly and paint on a design. If you use poster paints, give the dried maraca a coat of clear lacquer.

CLICKETY-CLACKER

Materials: a 1-by-2, 8″ long; 2 or 3 long dowels, ⅜″ in diameter; sandpaper; saw; Elmer's Glue.

Sand all the edges of the 1-by-2. Saw the dowels into 13 pieces, each 5″ long. Sand the ends and edges of each piece. Glue 12 pieces to the 1-by-2 as shown, applying glue to the dowels where they touch the wood and each other. Let them dry completely. Use the 13th piece of dowel as a striker—run it up and down the dowels or hit short, staccato strokes in 1 direction.

SIMPLE WEAVING

This small homemade loom produces a rectangular or square patch of weaving. The object is to make a lot of patches and sew them together into a wall hanging, coverlet or pillow. Or you can make 1 or 2 patches and sew them as decoration or pockets on clothing.

Materials: 1 small cardboard box; straight pins; comb with large teeth; yarn needle; ruler; weaving material—sport yarn, regular 4-ply yarn, cotton yarn, twine, string or any combination of these.

Open the box and fit the bottom into the top. Push pins into the short ends of the box at ¼″ intervals. Each pin should be anchored firmly in the center of the cardboard.

Warp the loom: Tie on yarn at a corner pin and bring the yarn back and forth, looping it around each pin. Pull the yarn taut as you warp, but not so taut that you pull the pins toward the center. Tie the yarn to the last pin.

Thread the yarn needle with a piece of weaving material at least 24″ long. Starting at the corner where you began warping, weave the yarn over and under across the warp. Leave about a 3″ tail of yarn at the beginning. Work back and forth across the warp in this manner, reversing the over-and-under pattern on each pass.

POINTERS

■ When you have used up the yarn or want to change color or type of weaving material, allow a couple of inches at the end of the strand and tie it to a new piece of yarn.

■ After each pass across the warp, beat back the yarn by holding the pins at the opposite end steady with your fingers and compressing the yarn with the teeth of the comb.

■ When you have finished each pass across the warp and start the next, don't pull the yarn too tight or you will pull the outside edges of the weaving toward the center.

■ Beat back as tightly as possible to get as many passes as possible across the warp.

When you have finished weaving, lift the patch carefully off the loom. Tie the loose ends at the beginning and end of the warp and at the beginning and end of the weaving to any part of the finished weaving. Do not worry about all the other loose ends. Just tuck these loose ends to what will be the wrong side when you sew one patch to another or to a piece of clothing.

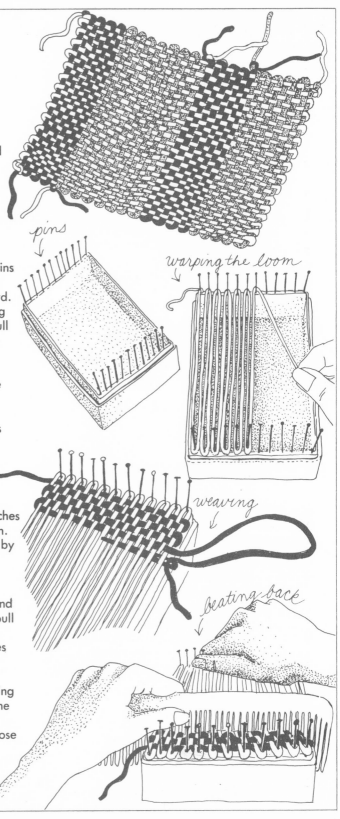

pins

warping the loom

weaving

beating back

THE BASICS OF RUG HOOKING

Materials: rug yarn; rug punch needle; 12 to 14 oz. (heavyweight) burlap; stretcher strips, two 24" long and two 18" long; liquid rubber; inexpensive paint brush, about 1½" wide; about 50 pushpins; ruler, scissors, felt tip pen.

1. Draw the outline of the rug on the burlap, keeping the outline parallel to the weave. Cut the burlap an eyeballed 4" outside the outline. Turn under the edge 1" and iron.

2. Draw the rug design and mark the color scheme on the burlap.

3. Put the stretcher strips together to make a frame. Fasten the burlap to it as tautly as possible with the pushpins as shown. The side of the rug that faces you will be the wrong side—your design comes out reversed.

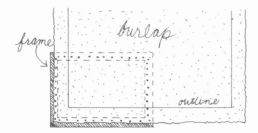

4. Roll the yarn into balls. Read the instructions that come with the punch needle and thread the needle accordingly. There should be a 2" strand coming out the end. Hold the needle like a pencil or, if there is a short handle, hold it with the handle pressed into the palm of the hand and the fingers on the shank. Work from left to right with the groove or slit in the needle facing the direction you are moving. If you have a choice of settings on the needle, begin with a middle one. The setting determines the length of the loops in the rug. You can adjust it later if you like.

Hold the frame in your lap with the back of it resting against a table. Experiment with the punch needle outside the outline of the rug. Hold the needle perpendicular to the burlap and push the needle between the threads. With your free hand, pull the end of the yarn through to the underside of the burlap. Raise the needle until it is just above the fabric, move it to the right two threads and push it down again until the handle touches the fabric. Raise the needle slowly until it is just above the fabric again, move it over 2 threads and plunge it down again. Keep punching the needle across the fabric to make loops. At the end of the row, or if you want to change colors, punch the needle through the burlap and cut the yarn <u>on the underside</u>.

When you can make loops with a fair degree of uniformity, you are ready to begin the rug.

5. (Working the rug) First punch the outlines of the smaller design areas. Fill in those areas with horizontal lines of loops. Then fill in the background areas, working horizontally from the bottom up.

When you have completed the section on the frame, pull out the pushpins, move the rug sideways and refasten it. When that is filled, move the rug down on the frame, then sideways, etc.

6. (Finishing the rug) Detach it from the frame. Pull out the yarn experimentation outside the outline. Turn the rug right side up and cut the yarn ends so they are even with the loops. Leave the loops as they are or cut them open to make a shag like this: slide a scissor blade into a row of loops and snip the whole lot open at the same time.

7. Cut the burlap edge to an eyeballed 2" outside the rug. Iron under the edges so that no unlooped burlap shows.

Apply one thin coat of liquid rubber to the back of the rug and the burlap edges. The rubber will glue down the turned-under burlap and keep the yarn loops from pulling out. Let it dry overnight.

FOUR DESIGNS FOR HOOKED RUGS

These designs can be adapted to rugs of 3 sizes—a small bath-size rug, 3' x 4½', or an area rug, either 4' x 6' or 5' x 7½'.

Draw the outline of the rug you plan to make on heavy-weight burlap. Rule the area off vertically into 9 sections of equal size and horizontally into 6 sections of equal size. Now you have a graph and can draw the design box by box.

Begin work with 10 skeins of rug yarn and buy more when you run out.

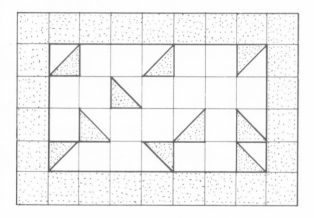 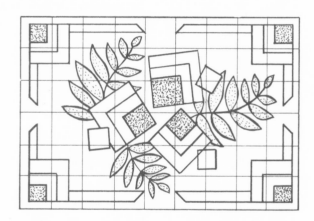

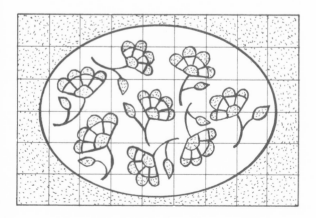 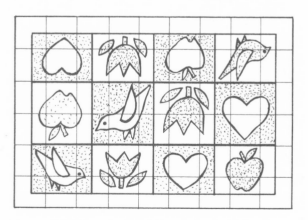

MEMORY LANE

PHOTO MONTAGE

A photo montage is a wonderful way to remember a special outing, vacation or time spent with one special person.

Collect a group of snapshots taken that day or during that time, a small picture frame and a piece of construction paper. Cut the paper to fit the frame. Then cut up the snapshots and arrange them in a montage on the construction paper or, if you like, on a doily that you have glued to the construction paper. The montage can be artful and serious or intentionally silly. For example, you might switch heads and bodies around, place people acrobatically on top of each other, exchange backgrounds so that an activity is taking place inappropriately. The outline of the montage can be uneven, symmetrical or in a special shape like a heart or diamond. When you like the arrangement, glue the montage down. When the glue has dried, put it in the frame.

MEMORY BOX

A memory box, a perfect anniversary or birthday gift, is a 3-dimensional diary created in a wooden box that is divided into compartments. Each compartment in the box depicts a different time and event in the person's life.

Craft and hobby shops sell the type of wooden box you need. It comes empty but already divided into compartments and has a glass top and hook on the back for hanging. All you have to do is fill it up.

For example, a memory box for grandparents might look like this. In one compartment is a picture of their wedding and a handful of rice. In another hangs a mirror on a string so they can see

themselves as they are. A third contains a photo of their children and grandchildren framed with a embroidered ribbon. A fourth compartment is filled with beads just for decoration, and a fifth has a photo and mementos of a place where they like to vacation.

A memory box gift from one teenager to another might, in one compartment, have objects taken from a favorite place, like sand and shells from a beach. In others, a school emblem or sports letter, photos of friends, a dance program and confetti, and perhaps the label from a favorite record.

Objects are either glued in place, hung from a string that is glued to the ceiling of a compartment, or just put in loose like rice, confetti or beans. The glass top will keep everything in its compartment when you hang the box.

SHADOW BOX

A shadow box is a 3-dimensional scrap book. When you take a trip, collect mementos all along the way: Tickets, matchbooks, foreign coins, postcards, road maps, envelopes or stamps from letters received, sightseeing brochures, pretty natural objects like pinecones, rocks, shells, driftwood. When you return home, arrange the items in a cardboard box that has been lined inside and out with construction paper or fabric. In the case of a map or sight-seeing brochure, you might want to cut out part of it rather than use the whole thing. When you like the arrangement, glue the objects in place. Glue a strand of ribbon around the outside of the box and staple the ends together. Hang the box on the wall from the ribbon.

GINGERBREAD FOLKS

Ingredients: ⅔ cup margarine; 1 cup packed brown sugar; 1¾ tsps. ginger; 1 tsp. cinnamon; ¼ tsp. ground cloves; 1½ tsps. salt; 1 egg; ⅓ cup molasses; 3 cups sifted flour; 1 tsp. baking soda; ½ tsp. baking powder.

Cream together the margarine, brown sugar, spices and salt. Add the egg and mix well; add the molasses and mix well.

Sift flour, soda and baking powder together. Add gradually to the molasses mixture, stirring until the dough is completely blended. Chill the dough in the refrigerator for 45 minutes.

Meanwhile, preheat the oven to 375° and grease 2 cookie sheets. Sprinkle the work surface generously with flour.

When the dough is chilled, break off ⅓ and roll it out on the floured surface to about 1/8'' thick. Keep rolling pin well-floured and sprinkle flour on the surface of the dough. Check under the dough to be sure it is not sticking to the work surface; sprinkle more flour if it is. Cut gingerbread folks with a cookie cutter and lift each cookie carefully onto a greased cookie sheet.

Continue to roll and cut the dough until the 2 sheets are full. Bake for 8-10 minutes. Cool on a wire rack. Repeat with the rest of the dough.

Decorate the cookies with frosting colored with food coloring. Use a decorating tube with a plain round tip.

Decorative Frosting
Ingredients: 3 tbsps. softened butter; 1½ cups confectioners sugar; dash of salt; 1 tsp. vanilla extract; 1½ tbsps. milk, cream or half-and-half; food coloring.

Cream the butter with half the sugar and milk. Add salt, vanilla and about half the remaining sugar. Continue beating. Add the remainder of the milk, beat it in and then add the last of the sugar. Beat the mixture until the frosting stands in stiff peaks when the beater is lifted out.

Divide the frosting into several small bowls and tint each a different color.

TRICK OR TREAT

For the young celebrators in the family—Halloween masks. Make the basic mask yourself as described below and then decorate it or hand it over to the trick or treater to decorate with a container of Elmer's Glue, scissors and an assortment of some of these ingredients: feathers, sequins, string, yarn, spangles, construction paper, rickrack, pipe cleaners, fabric scraps, beans, seeds, pasta, paper clips, aluminum foil, scraps of ribbon, buttons, autumn leaves, artificial flowers, corks.

THE BASIC MASK

On a stiff sheet of paper (bristol paper, oaktag or other from an art supply store), enlarge the graph to the increments indicated and draw the outline of the mask box by box. Cut out the mask. The graph side will be the wrong side of the mask.

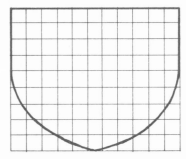

1 box = 1 sq. inch

Hold the mask over the face of the intended wearer. If it is too large, trim it down. With the mask in position over the face, mark the eyes, nose and mouth on the outside. Cut these out, checking the placement after each cutting. Punch or cut holes in the side of the mask and attach string through the holes so you can tie the mask on.

If you want a nose, cut the shape indicated out of construction paper, folding on the fold lines and glue it over the nose holes.

Pass these suggestions on to the decorator.

- Think 3-dimensionally. Decorations can pop off the face, dangle, stick straight up as well as lie flat.
- Combine textures and surfaces like shiny sequins and spangles or yarn, pasta, beans, seeds. You might cover the mask completely with a mosaic design.
- Consider creating an animal face as well as a fantasy face.
- Try unusual edges—pinked, torn, fringed, curled.
- Don't forget all the details and parts of a face—ears (place them in front of the stringing holes), cheeks, nose, eyebrows, eyelashes, moustaches, sideburns, beards.
- Curl construction paper to give the mask a curly head of hair, beard or eyelashes. Curl like this: Cut or tear strips of paper and wrap them tightly one at a time around a pencil or pull them across the blade of a scissors.
- More is better.

fold *bend & glue* *fold* *bend & glue*

FRIGHT WIGS

For a twist on the usual Halloween get-up, your child can disguise herself in a handmade wig. She will look like a cross between Shirley Temple and Harpo Marx.

Mopsy

A mop is worn on the head as shown. Cut the center front into bangs and arrange the rest of the mop into a mass of braids and pony tails tied with different-colored ribbons and yarns. Note: When you first put the mop on, there will be gaps at the sides. If you make a braid on each side containing some yarn from the front section of mop and some from the back, the gaps will disappear.

Flopsy

There are two ways to make this wig — with paper curls or store-bought fringe. In either case you make a cap, which will be the basis of the wig, by cutting off the sleeve of a t-shirt.

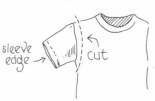

sleeve edge → cut

sleeve edge

turn edge under

Cut strips of construction paper. Curl the ends by rolling them up and securing for a few minutes with a paper clip. Staple the curls to the cap. Cut construction paper bangs and staple them on. Then sew up the opening at the sleeve edge of the cap.

For a head of fringe, sew up the sleeve edge of the cap first. Then sew a circle of fringe at the top of the cap and vertical strips all around.

MEXICAN YARN PAINTING

Mexican yarn paintings are colorful traditional folk art designs rendered on paper in a yarn mosaic. To find designs that would be suitable for your yarn painting, consult library books on Mexican folk art; or, if you would like a North American version of this craft, look in books on Pennsylvania Dutch folk art or Native American crafts.

Materials: scraps of yarn; wooden picture frame from the 5-and-10; a piece of pretty-colored poster board; Elmer's Glue; small paintbrush; paper cup.

Cut a piece of poster board to fit the frame. With a pencil and ruler, draw in a border 1″ from the edge. The yarn painting should not exceed that border so that the poster board can fit in the frame. Draw a simple folk art design or invent your own. Mark for colors if you want to plan ahead; otherwise, decide as you go along. Now fill in the picture completely with yarn. The basic technique is to dilute some glue in a paper cup with a few drops of water, paint on the glue and apply the yarn.

Pointers

◆ Before you begin, have your scraps of yarn cut into pieces—an assortment from 2″ to 12″ long. You will have to cut them down again to fit exactly, but at least they will be in manageable form.

◆ Be very free with color, changing frequently.

◆ Paint on glue and apply yarn in sections: first outline the parts of the painting; then fill in the parts, working out from the center when possible; finally do the background.

When you are filling in the parts of the painting and the background, be sure to place the strands of yarn right next to each other. No poster board should show between the strands.

When the painting is done, let the glue dry. Put the painting in the frame without the glass.

YO-YO QUILTING

Yo-yos are little puckered circles of cotton fabric that are pieced together into pillows and quilts. Like other native American crafts, yo-yo quilting, which was especially popular in the 1920s and 1930s, is enjoying a revival.

HOW TO MAKE A YO-YO

Materials: 1 scrap of soft cotton fabric; 1 cardboard disk, 4½" in diameter; needle and thread.

Draw around the disk on the wrong side of the fabric. Cut it out. Turn the edges in and pin a ¼" hem allowance. Sew the hem with a small running stitch and pull up the thread to gather tightly. Fasten off and flatten. A finished yo-yo should measure 2"-2¼" in diameter.

YO-YO PILLOWS

Make 72 yo-yos and sew them into 2 squares, each 6 yo-yos across x 6 down. Sew a square to each side of a pillow sham, 14" square. Stuff the sham with foam chips or Polyfil and sew up the end.

YO-YO QUILTS

A single bed quilt should measure 72" x 90"; a double bed quilt, 102" x 90". The amount of yo-yos you need for either quilt will vary because of the minute variations in the sizes of your yo-yos. Roughly, a single bed quilt will be 31-36 yo-yos across and 40-45 down. A double bed quilt will be 47-51 across and 40-45 down. When you sew the yo-yos together, try the quilt on the bed to fit it as it begins to approach the right size.

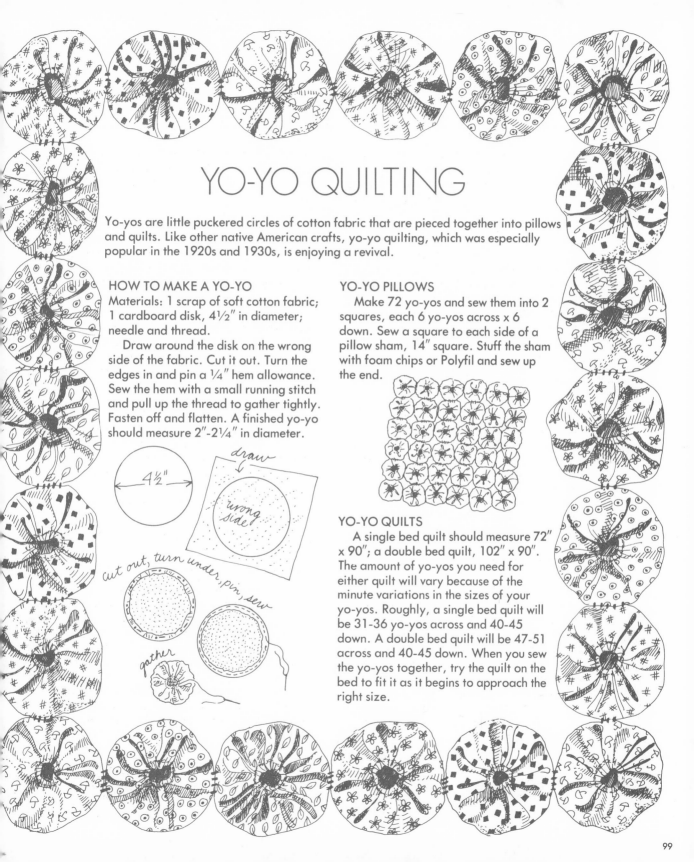

THE BASICS OF STENCILING

This early American decorative art was used to adorn walls, floors, furniture and small household objects with colorful repeating patterns. The technique described here is for stenciling on a small scale—pretty wooden boxes, trays, children's furniture, toys, picture frames—anything small that is made of unfinished wood, cardboard or paper.

Materials: brown paper bag; new single-edged razor blade or small pointed scissors; clear lacquer; soft brush to use with the lacquer; lacquer thinner to clean the brushes; poster paints and brushes to mix new colors; plate or tray to mix paints on; 1 small stencil brush, about ¼" in diameter (a stencil brush has stiff bristles cut flat across the top); scrap paper; a clean, dry object to be stenciled.

MAKING THE STENCIL

Cut unwrinkled, unfolded pieces of paper out of the paper bag. Paint each piece with clear lacquer. Let dry. Draw a pattern on the paper, centered, and cut it out with a razor blade or scissors. Use simple patterns that have very few tiny parts. Include connecting links within the design if you want to have cut-out parts within cut-out parts. If you would like different parts of the design to be different colors, cut separate stencils for each—e.g., a flower in one piece of paper and leaves in another.

PAINTING THE STENCIL PATTERN

Mix enough paint only for the stencil you are working with. Each time you change stencils, mix paint for the new one. Poster paint dries quickly on the palette, but can be restored with a drop or 2 of water. The paint should be thinned a bit from its natural consistency.

Important: Using a stencil brush is tricky at first so practice stenciling on scrap paper. Here's how to do it.

Dab the stencil brush around on the plate to get the bristles covered evenly with paint and to work off excess paint. Place the stencil over the scrap paper; hold it down firmly with your fingers or with straight pins. Paint the open areas of the stencil by making short, brisk strokes. Hold the stencil brush vertically and work from the cut edge of the stencil toward the middle. Quick, short strokes work much better than slow, drawn-out ones; they prevent the paint from seeping under the cut edges and blurring the image. You may have to make many strokes to build up the color density.

If the image persists in being blurred, you have (a) thinned the paint too much; (b) overloaded the brush with paint; (c) let the stencil wiggle or come up from the paper; (d) not used a brisk-enough stroke.

Each time you change paint colors, wash the stencil brush carefully. Use tepid water and soap, working the soap in by rubbing the bristles around in your palm.

COMPLETING THE STENCIL

When you have finished stenciling, it is very effective to add accents—painting them on with a regular, small, soft-bristle brush. Some possibilities: Add a darker edge to a design; outline one area; paint a line around the whole design; use some gold paint here and there.

Finally, when all stenciling and accenting is done, cover the object with a coat of clear lacquer. Use a soft brush and keep the strokes smooth.

SIX STENCIL PATTERNS

These patterns can be used in many combinations. Draw a ¼″ graph on paper bag stencil paper and draw in the patterns box by box. Cut the stencils and use them to paint designs on objects made of unfinished wood, paper or cardboard. Suggested objects: wooden tray; paper lampshade; knicknack shelf; flower box; children's chairs and table; wooden trinket box (available wherever decoupage supplies are sold); the frame of a mirror.

HOW TO MAKE TIN LANTERNS

Materials for one lantern: empty soup can; several inches of thin wire; 1 small candle
(a votive candle works well); aluminum foil; tin snips; hammer and large nail;
pliers; a piece of scrap wood to work on.

Remove both ends from soup can. Save one end. Remove the label from the can and scrub off the gluey residue underneath.

With the tin snips, cut the can open near the seam and flatten it out. Driving the nail from the inside of the can to the outside, hammer a pattern of holes in the can. Hammer two holes in each end of the can. With the tin snips, cut 1"-long slits along the top and bottom of the can. Bend out the cut edges.

Bend the can back into a cylindrical shape and wire it together, twisting the ends of wire on the inside. The lantern is completed.

Now make a holder for the candle out of the can top that you set aside. Cut ¼" snips around the perimeter of the can top. Use the pliers to turn up the edges. Anchor the candle in the center of the top with a few drops of melted wax. Set the top in three layers of aluminum foil cut into a round shape. Turn up the edges of the foil to catch the wax as it melts. Light the candle and place the lantern over it.

GIFTS OF FOOD

HERB VINEGAR

Either fresh or dried herbs will do nicely. If you use fresh ones, you will need 2 cups minced herbs per 1 quart vinegar. If you use dried ones, you will need 1½ tbsps. dried herbs per 1 quart scalded vinegar.

Put the herbs in a wide-mouthed jar. Bruise fresh herbs slightly with a wooden spoon and pour in the vinegar—cider, wine or white. Cover the jar tightly. Store the jar in a warm place for 10 days to 2 weeks and shake the jar vigorously every day. At the end of the time period, taste the vinegar for flavor. If the herb taste is strong enough, it's done. Strain the mixture, pour it into smaller bottles and label them. If the flavor is not strong enough, strain out the old herbs and repeat the process with new ones.

Suggested herbs to use: Sweet basil, thyme, marjoram, dill, rosemary, chives, mint, tarragon, fennel.

CURRY POWDER

Ingredients: 1 c. coriander seed; ⅓ c. red pepper flakes; ¼ c. poppy seed; ¼ c. cumin seed; ¼ c. mustard seed; ½ c. turmeric; 2 tbsps. garlic powder; 4 tbsps. salt.

Powder the seeds in a blender. Put the powder in a large bowl with the other ingredients and mix very well. Funnel into small jars or bottles and label.

SALAD DRESSING

To make one gift-sized jar of dressing, combine ¾ c. salad oil, ⅓ c. wine vinegar, 1 tsp. powdered mustard, 1 large clove of garlic cut into 4 slivers, ¼ tsp. salt and ¼ tsp. black pepper. Shake well and taste. If the dressing is not tangy enough, add a shake or 2 of salt. Remember—by the time you give or use the dressing, the garlic will have added flavor to the mixture. Label the jar.

HOLIDAY GREETING CARDS

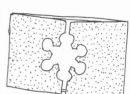

Materials: envelopes not larger than 6″ x 9″; assorted colors of construction paper; colored pencils; gummed stars; small piece of shirt cardboard; ruler; Elmer's Glue; scissors.

1. The cards, when they are folded, must be slightly smaller than the envelopes. To find out their size, make 2 calculations. Double the width of the envelopes and subtract ½″. This will be the width of the cards. Then subtract 1/8″ from the height of the envelopes. This will be the height of the cards. Cut construction paper to these dimensions—as many pieces as you want cards. Fold the ends of each strip of paper to meet in the middle.

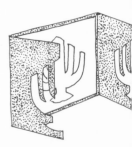

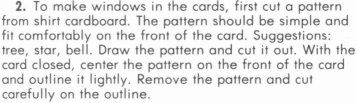

2. To make windows in the cards, first cut a pattern from shirt cardboard. The pattern should be simple and fit comfortably on the front of the card. Suggestions: tree, star, bell. Draw the pattern and cut it out. With the card closed, center the pattern on the front of the card and outline it lightly. Remove the pattern and cut carefully on the outline.

3. Cut a piece of construction paper slightly smaller than the main panel of the card. Open the window panels and glue the contrasting piece centered on the main panel. Close the window panel and outline the window with a colored pencil on the contrasting construction paper.

4. Decorate the outlined shape with gummed stars. Write the message and sign your name above and below the outlined shape.

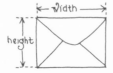

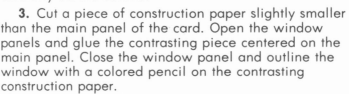

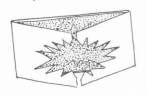

A MEXICAN CHRISTMAS

The highlight of Mexican Christmas festivities is the breaking of the piñata, a papier maché or earthenware animal or sphere filled with candy, charms and other tiny presents. The piñata, painted and gaily decorated with colored paper, hangs from the ceiling. One at a time, the children stand under the piñata. They are blindfolded, twirled around 3 times and then given 3 tries to break the piñata with a broomstick or other long stick.

Materials: 1 daily paper torn into scraps (approximately 2″ square, but just rip them—there is no need for accuracy); flour; water; 1 tube or jar of acrylic paint; a paintbrush; a spherical balloon; Vaseline; an empty flowerpot; colored tissue paper; Elmer's Glue.

To make a paste, put 1 cup flour in a bowl and add water, slowly, mixing, until the flour and water mixture is the consistency of thin pancake batter. Blow up the balloon, tie it and rub the surface with a thin coat of Vaseline. Place the balloon in the flowerpot, tied end down, balancing it so it stands alone. Dip individual pieces of newspaper in the paste to wet them completely and then apply them to the balloon. Cover the balloon with 1 layer of newspaper, overlapping the pieces. After you put each piece on, smooth it carefully over the balloon to make an even surface. The only part of the balloon that should remain uncovered is the small area that sits in the flowerpot.

As soon as you have applied the first coating of newspaper, apply two more. Let the papier maché dry completely. This may take 24 hours or longer. If you are in a hurry, put it in a warm oven (with the heat turned off) to speed the drying.

Pop the balloon, remove it and rub the inside of the papier maché ball with a rag to remove any Vaseline that sticks to it. Let dry another 24 hours.

Paint the piñata with 2 coats of acrylic paint. Then decorate it with tissue paper: Cut strips of tissue paper 1½″ wide; snip a 1″ fringe, curl the fringe carefully with a scissor blade; cut the strips down to 6″ lengths and glue them, overlapping, working up from the closed end of the piñata. Glue curled tissue paper streamers to the bottom of the piñata.

Put 3 holes around the rim of the piñata by pushing a nail through. Put string through the holes, fill the piñata with candy and presents, and hang it.

HOW TO MAKE
CHRISTMAS CANDLE HOLDERS

Christmas Trees

Use a tube of liquid solder (as glue) and 38 gauge decorator foil, which is very pretty soft aluminum, heavier than kitchen foil but completely pliable. Make each candle holder as follows.

Cut out 2 trees with scissors.

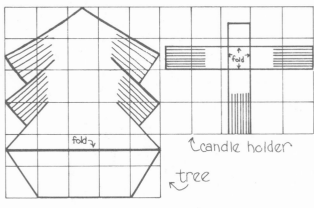

candle holder

tree

Cut the fringes and curl. Fold. Glue the trees back to back and decorate with small pieces of foil or sequins. Then cut out 2 candle holders. Cut fringe. Fold and glue each holder to a tree.

Place a small candle in the holder, using a few drops of wax to make it stick.

Pine cones

Break off the top piece of pine cone to make a niche for the candle. Glue the pine cone to a small square of corrugated cardboard that you have painted silver or gold or covered with pretty giftwrap paper. Drip hot wax into the niche and put candle in place.

HOW TO MAKE HOLIDAY SEALS

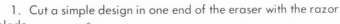

Holiday seals provide a festive touch to greeting cards, envelopes and gifts during the holiday season. You can make seals yourself with supplies from a stationery store and a batch of homemade, peppermint-flavored glue.

Materials: 1 gum or "Artgum" eraser for each stamp; 1 single-edged razor blade; paper in bright colors; ordinary office stamp pad in one or more colors; paint brush; ingredients for the glue—8 tbsps. white vinegar, 4 packets unflavored gelatin, 1 tbsp. peppermint extract.

1. Cut a simple design in one end of the eraser with the razor blade.

2. With a pencil and ruler, divide the sheets of paper into squares or rectangles that will accommodate the stamp comfortably, but not with room to spare.

3. Press the stamp on the stamp pad and practice printing it on scrap paper. The stamp need not be inked heavily to give a clear, crisp print. When you have mastered the technique, print the stamp in each ruled-off box on the colored paper, inking as required between stampings.

4. When all stamping is completed, make the gelatin glue. In a small saucepan, bring the vinegar to a boil. Add the unflavored gelatin, reduce to a low heat, and stir until the gelatin is completely dissolved. Add peppermint extract and mix it in well. You now have a little less than 1/2 cup glue, plenty for several sheets of paper.

5. Brush the glue on the back of the sheets of stamps. Use it sparingly. If the stamps are on thin paper, the paper may curl when you apply the glue. Do not worry. The stamps will straighten out just fine when you lick and apply them.

If the glue in the pan begins to harden while you are brushing it on, place the saucepan in a large pan of hot water and let the glue soften. If you want to save leftover glue for another time or use, pour the remainder into a bottle and cap it. The glue should last several months.

6. Let the sheets of stamps dry completely. Cut out the stamps along the pencil lines. When you want to use a stamp, just lick the back and stick it on.

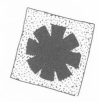

HOW TO MAKE RAINBOW WRAPPING PAPER

Materials: tableau paper (sold at art supply stores) or a similar lightweight, absorbent paper; food coloring; newspapers.

Mix dyes—water and food coloring—in shallow containers like the compartments of a muffin tin. Make the colors as light or intense as you like by the addition of a little or a lot of water. Fill one container with plain water.

Fold the paper like an accordion into a long strip, creasing the edges firmly. Then fold like an accordian into squares or triangles. Work with paper in any size up to about 24" x 24".

Print a design by dipping the corners of the folded paper into dye, utilizing one or a combination of the following techniques.

■ Dip 1 or more corners into a different dye color.
■ Dip 1 or more corners into water first and then into dye. The water makes the color spread and produces a feathery print.
■ Dip 1 corner into water only and the opposite corner into water and dye.
■ Hold a corner firmly with your thumb and forefinger when you dip it in dye, or in water and then dye. The color will run up the edges of the paper and leave the place where you are holding the paper without color.

Put the folded paper between several sheets of newspaper on the floor and press down on them with your foot. Take out the paper and open it out carefully. Let the paper dry on newspaper.

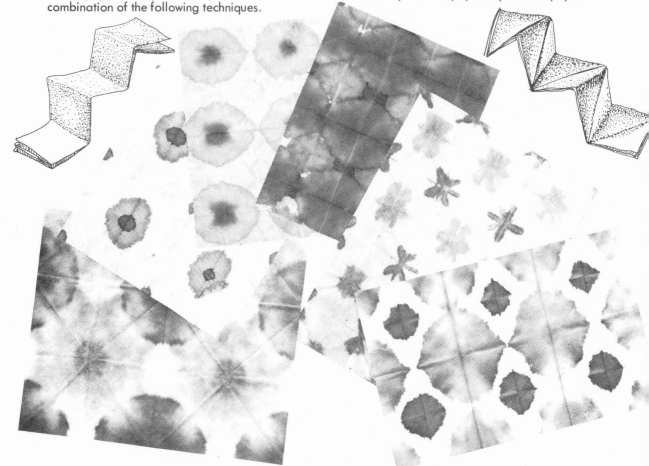

THE TWELVE-DAYS-OF-CHRISTMAS ORNAMENTS

12 LADIES DANCING: Make a cone of pretty paper with paper arms for the body; use a wooden bead with yarn hair for the head. Paint a face on the bead. Trim the skirt with something fancy—ruffles, lace, or sequins.

11 LORDS A-LEAPING: Make the lords from gingerbread men decorated with white frosting. Hang with a bit of yarn.

10 DRUMMERS DRUMMING: Paint a 3" section of cardboard tube (cut it from a paper towel tube). Glue circles of fabric to each end; trim with ribbon and yarn. Add a yarn loop for hanging.

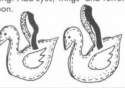

9 PIPERS PIPING: Pipes of Pan are made from dowels, 3/8" in diameter. Cut 6 pieces of dowel—each should be 1/4" longer than the one before, starting with a dowel 1 1/2" long. Glue them together and paint silver. Glue on a ribbon and hang.

8 MAIDS A-MILKING: Cut paper dolls with milk cans and string them from branch to branch like garlands.

7 SWANS A-SWIMMING: For each bird, cut 2 identical birds from white felt. Sew together 3/4 of the way around and stuff with cotton. Finish sewing. Add eyes, wings and velvet ribbon.

6 GEESE A-LAYING: Blow out the insides of small raw eggs. Paint gold and hang with a bead and gold thread.

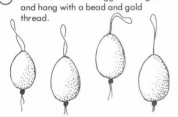

5 GOLD RINGS: With gold cord, tie together 5 gold-colored curtain rings, 3/4"-1 1/2" in diameter.

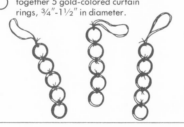

4 COLLIE BIRDS: Make the head, body, and wing from stiff paper and join together with paper fasteners. Glue each bird to a clothespin and pin to the tree.

3 FRENCH HENS: For each bird, cut 2 identical birds from colored paper. Glue feathers to one and glue the other over it. Hang with yarn.

2 TURTLEDOVES: Buy a small package of self-setting clay (it hardens without firing). Shape it into small doves and pierce with a large needle. Let them dry, paint and sprinkle with glitter. Thread on a bright-colored string.

and A PARTRIDGE IN A PEAR TREE:
Twist pipecleaners to make a small tree with branches. Glue on felt leaves, pears, and, naturally, a partridge.

12 WAYS TO WRAP A PRESENT

■ Make a paper bag or envelope out of fancy wrapping paper or a drawstring bag out of cloth. Put the gift inside.

■ Wrap the present simply or not at all and place it inside something special like a flowerpot, brandy snifter, antique tin, basket, decoupage box or goldfish bowl.

■ Use unusual wrapping paper—road maps, colored Sunday comics, tissue paper, patterned shelf paper, marbleized paper, rice paper, flint paper (or other glossy paper from an art supply store), plain brown paper from a paper bag that has been cut open and ironed smooth, rainbow wrapping paper.

■ Decorate the wrapping with a snapshot, gummed seals from a stationery store or pictures cut from magazines.

■ Tie the package with a variegated yarn, metallic yarn, rug yarn, chenille, jute twine or pink nylon string. Consider using several kinds or colors of yarn together on one package or braiding the yarns.

■ Tie the package with something unexpected—rickrack, ball fringe or metallic braid.

■ Tie the package with a fancy embroidered or taffeta ribbon that can be used afterward as a hair ribbon or clothing trim.

■ Decorate the package with something natural—a pine cone, sprig of holly, mistletoe, shells, assortment of dried herbs or grasses, a peacock feather.

■ Tie the bow on the box around a real, dried, silk or fabric flower.

■ Top the wrapping with a silly stocking stuffer—a party hat, noisemaker, tiny game or puzzle or balloon.

■ Top the wrapping with a tiny extra gift—a small sewing kit, roll of film, deck of cards, sachet, cigar, special soap, lipstick, handkerchief, address or date book, box of crayons, package of appliqués.

■ Top the wrapping with something festive—bells, ornaments, doilies wrapped around paper flowers, glitter, tinsel or yarn pompom.

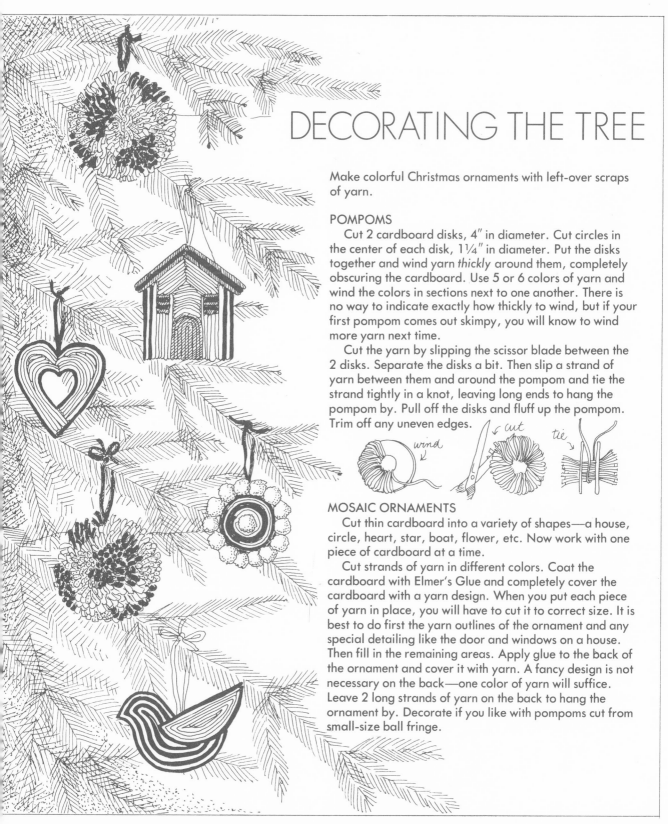

DECORATING THE TREE

Make colorful Christmas ornaments with left-over scraps of yarn.

POMPOMS

Cut 2 cardboard disks, 4″ in diameter. Cut circles in the center of each disk, 1¼″ in diameter. Put the disks together and wind yarn *thickly* around them, completely obscuring the cardboard. Use 5 or 6 colors of yarn and wind the colors in sections next to one another. There is no way to indicate exactly how thickly to wind, but if your first pompom comes out skimpy, you will know to wind more yarn next time.

Cut the yarn by slipping the scissor blade between the 2 disks. Separate the disks a bit. Then slip a strand of yarn between them and around the pompom and tie the strand tightly in a knot, leaving long ends to hang the pompom by. Pull off the disks and fluff up the pompom. Trim off any uneven edges.

MOSAIC ORNAMENTS

Cut thin cardboard into a variety of shapes—a house, circle, heart, star, boat, flower, etc. Now work with one piece of cardboard at a time.

Cut strands of yarn in different colors. Coat the cardboard with Elmer's Glue and completely cover the cardboard with a yarn design. When you put each piece of yarn in place, you will have to cut it to correct size. It is best to do first the yarn outlines of the ornament and any special detailing like the door and windows on a house. Then fill in the remaining areas. Apply glue to the back of the ornament and cover it with yarn. A fancy design is not necessary on the back—one color of yarn will suffice. Leave 2 long strands of yarn on the back to hang the ornament by. Decorate if you like with pompoms cut from small-size ball fringe.